KANAKA

KANAKA

The Untold Story
of Hawaiian Pioneers
in British Columbia and
the Pacific Northwest

Tom Koppel

Whitecap Books
Vancouver/Toronto

The information in this book is true and complete to the best of our knowledge. All
recommendations are made without guarantee on the part of the author or Whitecap
Books Ltd. The author and publisher disclaim any liability in connection with the use
of this information. For additional information please contact Whitecap Books Ltd.,
351 Lynn Avenue, North Vancouver, BC, V7J 2C4.

Edited by Elizabeth McLean
Cover and interior design by Warren Clark
Cover photograph courtesy of Salt Spring Island Archives
Typeset by Warren Clark

Printed and bound in Canada.

Canadian Cataloguing in Publication Data
Koppel, Tom.
  Kanaka

  Includes bibliographical references and index.
  ISBN 1-55110-295-1
  1. Hawaiians—British Columbia. 2. Hawaiians—Northwest, Pacific. 3. British
  Columbia—History—19th century.* 4. Northwest, Pacific—History. I. Title.

FC3850.H38K66 1995   971.1'004994   C94-910956-8
F1089.7.H38K66 1995

Acknowledgements

I had help, encouragement, and support from many people and institutions in researching and writing this book. I am particularly indebted to Professor Jean Barman of the University of British Columbia, who shared vital research materials that she had gathered in Hawaii and elsewhere. Generous financial support came from the minister of state for multiculturalism and citizenship and from the Royal Canadian Geographical Society. I enjoyed the cooperation of many research sources, but especially the staffs at the Hudson's Bay Company Archives (HBCA)/Provincial Archives of Manitoba (PAM), the Provincial Archives of British Columbia (PABC), B.C. Archives and Records Service (BCARS), the City of Vancouver Archives (CVA), and the Salt Spring Island Archives.

I want to thank the Island Savings Credit Union for lending me a microfilm viewer, and the Mary Hawkins Memorial Library for providing space to use it.

Other researchers, writers, editors, publishers, archive personnel, and interested individuals who gave me information, documents, photos, letters of reference, or simply encouragement and inspiration are: Judith Andersen, Richard Andersen, Chris Arnett, Judith Beattie, Randy Bouchard, Roscoe Buckland, Ross Clark, Cathy Collins, Ian Darragh, Mary Davidson, Dorothy Dodds, Terry Glavin, Carol Haber, Michael Halleran, Beth Hill, Dorothy Hill, Marlyn Horsdal, Yvonne Klan, Frieda Klippenstein, Melia Lane, Shirley Larden, Shirley Morrison, Jamie Morton, Momilani Naughton, Peggy Nicholls, Helen Norton, John Porter, Marie Reidke, Roger Roberts, Andrew Scott, Joan Thornley, Bob Tyrrell, Bruce Watson, Howard White, Elvi Whittaker, Dick Wilson, Jean Wilson, Ann Witty, Brian Young, and William Young.

Finally, I owe thanks to many descendants of the Kanakas (and their immediate families) for granting me interviews, passing on family letters and photos, and generally allowing me to poke around in their lives and those of their ancestors. They include Lonny Bate, Larry Bell, Violet Bell, Jackie Hembruff, Pauline Hillaire, Tom Johnston, Karey Litton, Mabel McFee, Wendy Maurer, Donna Miranda, Carey Myers, Gerald Nahanee, James Nahanee, Teresa O'Leary, Harry Roberts, Sherry Roberts, Laura Roland, and Ruth Ullrich.

Needless to say, I am fully responsible for any errors or omissions in the text.

Contents

Introduction

Mention Hawaii and most people on the Northwest Coast picture coconut palms swaying in tropical breezes, a paradise that we reach by jumbo jet for a brief respite from the northern winter. From our viewpoint it is a distinctly one-way relationship. Who would guess that natives of that sun-blessed archipelago would willingly leave their climate and society to live in ours? Yet during the nineteenth century, in one of the least-known migrations in North American history, scores of Hawaiians came to what is now coastal British Columbia and the Pacific Northwest, put down roots, and stayed.

Imagine that we could jump back more than one hundred years to the 1880s in British Columbia's scenic Gulf Islands, which nestle in the sheltered waters between mountainous Vancouver Island and the North American mainland. On the southern end of Salt Spring Island, the largest of the group, and on several adjacent islands, we would encounter a population of hardy Hawaiian pioneer homesteaders living in rough log cabins on recently cleared land. They called themselves (and were called by others) Kanakas, the Hawaiian word for "person" or "human being."[1]

These Kanakas eked out a subsistence living through dawn-to-dusk toil, as did most of their equally poor island neighbours, a motley group that included whites, blacks from the United States, and many of mixed (part native Indian) blood. But in some ways the Kanakas were unique. They held *luau* feasts on the beaches of their adopted islands, were partial to imported *poi* (a traditional dish made from fermented taro root), played Hawaiian music on the ukulele, danced the hula, and fished according to their old methods.

A smaller group of Kanakas could have been found on the shores of Coal Harbour in what is today the West End of metropolitan Vancouver. Three families lived at the "Kanaka Ranch," a cluster of houses, outbuildings, and cherry trees near a creek, where the posh Westin Bayshore Hotel now stands at the foot of Denman Street. Across Burrard Inlet at Moodyville (today's North Vancouver), there was a Kanaka Row whose dark-skinned residents worked at the large sawmill. Even earlier, in the 1860s, there was a Kanaka Row (now called Humboldt Street) in the provincial capital,

1

Victoria, facing what was then a stinking mud flat but is now (thanks to landfill) the site of the venerable Empress Hotel.

There were perhaps ten families on the shores of the Fraser River in the Maple Ridge area and a smaller group who had intermarried and joined the Indians at Tsawwassen, south of Vancouver. The chief of the Songhees Indians of southern Vancouver Island was, himself, part Kanaka. All along the inner coast of British Columbia we might encounter individual Kanaka men, most of them married to native Indian women, working seaside home-steads or at sawmills or canneries, or on commercial ships. And there were Kanakas who had intermarried with the Lummi Indians of nearby Wash-ington Territory.

Like any other ethnic group, these Hawaiians included heroes and villains. Some became esteemed members of their local communities. Oth-ers were sent to the gallows for murder. But mainly they were adventurous people who had chosen to leave their homeland and take their chances with frontier life in a foreign land. Gutsy survivors, they worked hard, raised families, and adapted remarkably well to their new home.

I first learned of this unique thread in the diverse ethnic fabric of the Northwest when I signed on as winter caretaker of tiny Russell Island, half a mile south of Salt Spring Island. I discovered that its first owner, a fruit grower named William Haumea, had been a pure-blooded Hawaiian. As late as 1960 an old, part-Kanaka descendant named "Uncle Abel" Douglas had made his home there. His mother, a beautiful and feisty woman named Maria Mahoy—she was probably half Kanaka, half Indian—had raised a large family on the island and passed on to her children a rich blend of Hawaiian, native Indian, and mainstream Anglo-Canadian beliefs, values, and traditions. Her grandchildren and great-grandchildren still return to Russell Island for the occasional visit.

Then someone pointed out Jack Roland, since deceased, who worked on the Salt Spring Island ferry and whose facial features were distinctly Hawaiian. His brother Paul had already told their family tale to local his-tory buffs and journalists, and had been treated to a headline-making trip to Hawaii by a major Honolulu newspaper. On Salt Spring Island itself there was a Kanaka Road in the main village of Ganges. Also in Ganges was the Kanaka Place Restaurant, whose owner, a Kanaka descendant named Jackie Hembruff, had printed a brief history of the local Hawaiian community on the back of her menus. I learned that the log cabin where a friend of mine lived had been built by an early Kanaka settler. (It is still standing, in reasonably good condition, more than a century later.) When I visited nearby Portland Island, another island that had been settled by Hawaiians and is today a provincial marine park, I followed the Kanaka Trail to Kanaka Bluff. A few years later, at Newcastle Island near the city of Nanaimo on Vancouver Island, I sat alone on the beach at Kanaka Bay and pondered the fate of "Kanaka Pete" Kakua, who was buried there after being hanged for murder.

It gradually became apparent that there had been a sizeable Hawaiian population on the Northwest Coast, but that little was known about it. Several books and articles on Salt Spring Island history told bits of the tale, but none was thoroughly researched. It was clear that many—probably most—of the Kanakas had come to B.C. while working for the Hudson's Bay Company (HBC) as "servants" in the fur trade.

But the certainties ended there. Had some jumped from passing ships, as one colourful account claimed, and swum ashore to islands that, allegedly, reminded them of home? Had they been given their land by the HBC for their years of service, as some descendants believed? Had some returned home to the Hawaiian Islands and then chosen to come back to B.C. to settle? Were they a coherent group, with a leader, or a rag-tag band of individual settlers? To what extent had they retained their Hawaiian language and customs while living as pioneers on what was still a sparsely inhabited coast? And what had become of their descendants?

When I began to research the topic, I was surprised to find how little had been written about these people. Although in the mid-1850s they constituted around ten percent of the non-native population of the Colony of Vancouver Island, most histories of the Northwest and of the Hudson's Bay Company gave them at best a footnote or two. Some failed to mention them at all.[2] Digging further, though, I discovered a wealth of scattered information in public records and archives. I worked through the employment records of the Hudson's Bay Company to get a more accurate idea of the numbers of people involved and to trace the careers of key individuals. And I met Kanaka descendants who were eager to tell their family stories. Gradually I pieced together a tale that was intriguing in its own right and that shed new light on the early history of British Columbia and the Pacific Northwest.

I

Terra Incognita

A surprising fact about the Age of Discovery is how late Hawaii remained unknown to western mariners. Magellan's fleet, after all, crossed the vast Pacific wastes in 1521 on the first circumnavigation of the globe. Yet more than two and one-half centuries were to pass before Captain James Cook chanced to sight the high volcanic peaks of the extensive and populous Hawaiian archipelago. During that time nearly all of what today we call the Pacific Rim was explored, along with many of the Pacific's major island groups. Much of the west coasts of North and South America were mapped, claimed, and colonized by Spain. The remote Alaskan coast was explored by Russia in the 1740s, and trading posts established. In 1774 the first Spanish ship made a landfall on the west coast of Vancouver Island. Even the Antarctic continent was discovered by Cook, on his second voyage, five years earlier than Hawaii.

Through most of the eighteenth century, then, Hawaii, with its population of some 300,000, remained one of the most self-contained, culturally isolated major societies on earth. Separated by two thousand miles of ocean from the nearest large island group or continent, Hawaiians can have had only the dimmest awareness that peoples other than themselves existed. The islands had been settled at least one thousand years earlier in the latter stages of the colonization of the mid- and eastern Pacific by Polynesian sailors. Occasional canoe voyages may have kept Hawaii in contact with ethnically related island groups, such as the Marquesas and Society Islands to the south, whence their ancestors had come. But, although it is conceivable that individual Hawaiian vessels strayed eastward to North America— or that North American Indians made the trip in the other direction—there is no hard evidence that this happened. It is even less likely that round trips were made. Thus the Northwest Coast was, presumably, terra incognita to the peoples of Hawaii until the last quarter of the eighteenth century.

This changed quickly after January 18, 1778, when Captain Cook, on his third and last great voyage, reached the Hawaiian Islands, landing on the island of Kauai and naming the group the Sandwich Islands (after his patron, the Earl of Sandwich). Cook took on fresh water and food for the onward voyage in search of the elusive "Straits of Anian" or Northwest Passage. He failed to find it, but did cruise along the coast of what is today British Columbia and Alaska, stopping at Nootka on the west coast of Vancouver Island and acquiring soft black sea otter pelts. When he returned to the Sandwich Islands he was killed by a mob of Hawaiians in a skirmish at Kealakekua Bay on the Kona Coast of the Big Island of Hawaii. (Only part of his dismembered body was recovered, which led to the belief that he had been cannibalized. True or not, this was to have darkly humorous echoes for the Kanakas on the Northwest Coast.)

After Cook's ships departed, no foreign vessels seem to have stopped in the Islands until 1786, when two British and two French ships visited. But Cook's men had sold their Nootka furs for high prices at Canton. And word of fur sales in China by Russian traders from Alaska had filtered back to Europe and the Yankee ports of New England. When expeditions to exploit this Northwest Coast fur trade were organized, the Sandwich Islands became a natural mid-ocean way station. Hawaii had water and an abundance of breadfruit, sweet potatoes, yams, and coconuts. In fact, given the prevailing winds and currents in the North Pacific, it was difficult in the days of square-riggers to round Cape Horn and reach the Northwest Coast (or cross the Pacific from China) without sailing close to those lush shores. With its balmy climate and inviting women, Hawaii was also an ideal spot for vessels engaged in the fur trade to spend the winter. Virtually all ships heading for the Northwest Coast stopped there, and many took on passengers.

The first to do so was the *Imperial Eagle,* commanded by British Captain Charles Barkley, but flying the Austrian flag to circumvent the East India Company's trade monopoly. It reached Hawaii in May 1787 and, according to its log, traded nails to the natives in exchange for hogs "at the rate of a large nail per head." Before it sailed for the Northwest Coast there "came alongside several canoes with fishs. One of the natives remained on board, signifying an inclination to go in the ship."[1] This was a young woman

Early Honolulu.
Lithograph by Adam from a drawing by Choris. (HBCA/PAM 1987/363-H-27/2/N11683)

named Winee, who became the personal servant of Frances Barkley, the captain's wife, and the first Hawaiian known to have visited the Northwest Coast.

Other Hawaiians, impressed with the Western visitors, their ships and technology, and their tales of distant lands, were equally curious and adventurous. And despite the prevalent condescension of the age, the Europeans were also impressed with their Hawaiian guests' innate intelligence and personal dignity. In August 1787 a chief named Tianna (also written Ka-i'ana) left the Islands with Captain John Meares's ship *Nootka,* which belonged to the British-owned Bengal Fur Company. Tianna's grandson went to California in 1839, and his descendants live there to this day (see Chapter 4). The same year other ships took two other Hawaiians to China, in Meares's words "rather as objects of curiosity, than from the better motive of instruction to them, or advantage to commerce."[2]

Winee went on to China following the *Imperial Eagle's* successful trading season on the Northwest Coast and was left at Macao to return to Hawaii. She found passage with Meares, who praised her as possessing "virtues that are seldom to be found in the class of her Countrywomen to which she belonged; and a portion of understanding that was not to be expected in a rude and uncultivated mind."[3] Meares described Tianna as a man with an "air of distinction,"[4] and with "capacities which education might have nurtured into intellectual superiority."[5]

Unfortunately, both Winee and Tianna fell ill. Meares wrote,

Our friends of Owyhee had suffered extremely during the passage across the China seas . . . the poor, unfortunate woman justified our fears concerning her, that she would never again see her friends or native land. She died February 5. [1788] At noon her body was committed to the deep; nor was it thought an unbecoming act to grace her remains with the formalities of that religion [Christianity] which opens wide its arms to the whole human race.[6]

Tianna recovered and, on board Meares's sister ship *Iphigenia Nubiana* (under Captain William Douglas), eventually made the voyage to Nootka. Meares's account gives a first look at the complex three-way relationship of whites, Hawaiians, and native Northwest Coast Indians that would play such a large role in the Kanaka experience in North America. When Tianna met the Nootka Chief Maquinna, the latter took an instant dislike to him, in Meares's opinion because Tianna was so much taller. And Tianna returned the sentiment, allegedly because of the Indians' small stature and presumed practice of cannibalism.

There is already a sense here of the "middling" status that Hawaiians would have on the Northwest Coast throughout the nineteenth century. As servants in the fur trade and dark-skinned "natives," they would stand a good notch below European and American whites in the social pecking order. But at the same time they were favoured by whites over the Northwest Coast Indians. One white observer after another commented favourably on the Hawaiians' impressive stature, good looks, lively intelligence, intellectual curiosity, and personal cleanliness.

This ranking of Hawaiians below whites but several degrees above Indians worked in favour of the Kanakas from an early date and affected their employment opportunities and marriage patterns for at least a

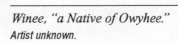

Winee, "a Native of Owyhee."
Artist unknown.

Tiana (Ka-i'ana), "a prince of Atooi."
Artist unknown. (HBCA/PAM 1987/363-H-27/1/ N11682)

century. Some Europeans even viewed Polynesians romantically as innocent but superior beings—the "noble savage." Of course, unlike the Indians, who vastly outnumbered the fur traders and early settlers, the Hawaiians, a minority on the Northwest Coast, were never a danger to white society. In fact, they were often employed to defend HBC posts and white settlers against the threat of Indian attack.

In Hawaii, taking Islanders on board commercial vessels soon became a common practice. In 1789 the Yankee captain Robert Gray, who discovered the mouth of the Columbia River, took Chief Attoo with him back to Boston. In 1789 another American skipper, Captain Ingraham, who was trading furs from Nootka to Canton, took a crown prince named Opye with him to Boston, returning him to Hawaii in 1791. In 1792 the British ship *Jenny* sailed to Nootka Sound with two Hawaiian women. They returned home in 1794 with Captain George Vancouver, who had the distinct impression that they had been taken against their will.

Not all male Hawaiian passengers went as guests, either. In many cases, by the time a ship reached the Islands illness and desertions had created crew shortages. Eventually, Hawaiians began to sign on to work as extra hands. In 1807 two young men, Hopoo and Obookiah, joined Captain John Brintnall of New Haven, Connecticut, as cabin boy and sailor respectively. They went to New York and were taken in to live with families. Hopoo later served on an American ship in the War of 1812, and was captured by the British in the West Indies. Both Obookiah and Hopoo later began studies for the ministry in New England. Obookiah translated the book of Genesis into Hawaiian and began to work on a Hawaiian grammar, dictionary, and spelling book, but he fell ill with typhus and died. Hopoo, however, returned to Hawaii in 1819 and helped establish the first Protestant mission at Honolulu. Decades later he went to California to join the Gold Rush.

Despite Captain Cook's violent demise and subsequent attacks on visiting ships, in time foreign ships came to be received in Hawaii with considerable hospitality. This was due, in part, to a bloody domestic Hawaiian struggle for power in which Western technology and know-how were extremely useful. Kamehameha, an ambitious young chief from the Big Island who was probably present at Cook's death, set out to conquer his rival chieftains. In 1789 he obtained small arms and ammunition from Captain Douglas, as well as a powerful swivel gun that he mounted on the platform of a large double canoe. Kamehameha saw these foreigners, with their powerful weapons and knowledge, as convenient allies and provided them with luxurious accommodations, the best food, and wives from the class of nobles. White sailors, some of whom had begun as his captives, rose to become esteemed advisers.

By 1811, twenty to thirty Europeans and Americans had been encouraged to settle in the Islands. With their help, and with considerable bloodshed, Kamehameha united the Islands into a kingdom with many of the institutions (and even the grandiose trappings) of European monarchies. The breakdown of the traditional, extremely hierarchical society, with its strict taboos (*kapus*) and other quasi-religious beliefs and practices, was then very rapid. By the early 1840s, when Herman Melville still found the Marquesas idyllic, Honolulu and Lahaina were already the busiest ports in the Pacific Islands. As one history of Hawaii notes: "Honolulu grew to be one of the liveliest and most dissolute complexes of grog shops and sailors' whorehouses in the world."[7]

2

We Kill Every Man
You Bid Us

By the early years of the nineteenth century, the maritime fur trade was firmly established along the Northwest Coast, from northern California to the Aleutian Islands. When Lewis and Clark wintered near the mouth of the Columbia River in 1805 to 1806, they narrowly missed meeting the Boston ship *Lydia* and found that the local Chinook Indians already possessed a wide variety of Western trade goods. British and American ships also traded regularly with coastal Indians at Nootka Sound and the Queen Charlotte Islands and often wintered in Hawaii. Except in Alaska, however, where the Russians had permanent trading posts, this was at best a sporadic, catch-as-catch-can system of trade. Ships might appear suddenly at a sheltered anchorage with goods to offer. But the Indians had no way of knowing for certain when to show up with their furs. Neither could the ship-borne traders be sure that the furs they sought would be available.

The man who changed this was John Jacob Astor, a German-born New York real estate tycoon who became a major player in the lucrative, globe-girdling China trade. Ships from the Northwest Coast would load up with sea otter pelts (worth up to $100 each at Canton), perhaps top up with valuable sandalwood in Hawaii, and sail to China. Having sold the cargo, they would buy Chinese tea, silk, porcelain, and spices for sale in New York, then reload with trinkets, knives, pans, blankets, and rum, which would be taken around Cape Horn to the Northwest Coast and traded to the Indians for more furs. Astor hoped to dominate this trade (and head off the plans by the rival British-owned North West Company to gain a foothold on the coast) by establishing a permanent post at the mouth of the Columbia River. The Columbia's vast drainage basin, which included such impor-

Astoria or Fort George on the Columbia River.
(Columbia River Maritime Museum 1979*49*10)

tant tributaries as the Willamette and Snake rivers, was still largely unexploited and was subject to conflicting British and American claims. To the south was Spanish California. To the north was Russian Alaska. In between was some of the best fur country on the Pacific coast, ripe for exploitation.

Astor founded the Pacific Fur Company and dispatched the first ship, the barque *Tonquin,* to establish the fortified trading post called Astoria. The *Tonquin,* under Captain Jonathan Thorn with a ship's company of thirty-three sailors, clerks, partners, and experienced canoeists, was to be followed a year later by a second Astor ship, the *Beaver* (not to be confused with the later Hudson's Bay Company steamship *Beaver*). Thorn was a brutal tyrant, and when his ship reached Hawaii in 1811 some of the crew deserted. At Honolulu he decided to bolster his forces. As one shipboard observer wrote,

> for the services of the Establishment [i.e. the fort] we engaged twelve Islanders, the term of their contract being three years, during which time we undertook to feed and clothe them and at the expiration of their contract, to give them goods to the value of one hundred piastres. The Captain took on twelve others for the work of the ship. These people make reasonably good sailors, seemed eager to enter our service and we could have engaged more of them.[1]

The *Beaver,* when it arrived in May 1812, brought an additional twenty-six Kanakas to work at Astoria.

One reason Thorn was glad to hire Kanakas was for their superb swimming, diving, and boat-handling abilities, which he realized would be a great asset on the rivers and coastal waters of North America. "Remarkable for their skill in managing light craft and able to swim and dive like waterfowl," was how the Astor men viewed them.[2]

Nearly all Hawaiians at the time lived close to the sea, bathed several times a day, and were as at home in the water as on land. As early as 1787 Captain Barkley's wife had noted of Hawaiian women: "Their dexterity in swimming is most surprising. They are quite equal to the men in the Art, and cannot be distinguished from them in the Water; it is a disgusting sight."[3] While the *Tonquin* was still in Hawaii, two Islanders, offered a reward by Captain Thorn, dove to retrieve some ship's blocks that had fallen overboard. On one dive they stayed underwater a full four minutes. "This exercise seemed to exhaust them, to such an extent that blood was flowing freely from the nose and ears of one of them."[4] Even so, they finally did bring up the hardware.

A later American observer was equally impressed after watching Kanakas launch and land small boats on exposed beaches in heavy surf:

> . . . the heavy swell of the Pacific was setting in, and breaking in loud and high "combers" on the beach. . . . [The boatload of Sandwich Islanders] gave a shout, and taking advantage of a great comber which came swelling in . . . they gave three or four long and strong pulls, and went in on top of the great wave, throwing their oars overboard, and as far from the boat as they could throw them, and jumping out the instant that the boat touched the beach, and then seizing hold of her and running her up high and dry upon the sand.[5]

The *Tonquin*'s Kanakas proved their value at the very first encounter with North American sea conditions, when the ship ran into trouble at the treacherous Columbia River bar in March 1811. Two whaleboats were sent out to take soundings, but an ebbing tide and fearful breaking seas prevented them from returning to the ship. One boat, with seven men, was lost for good. The other, which included two Kanakas in its crew, was swamped, and two white men were lost. A third later reported how the Kanakas saved his life:

I kept tossing about at the mercy of the waves. While in this state I saw the two Sandwich Islanders struggling through the surf to get hold of the boat, and being expert swimmers they succeeded. After long struggles they got her turned upon her keel, bailed out some of the water, and recovered one of the oars. I made several attempts to get near them, but the weight of my clothes and the rough sea had almost exhausted me. I could scarcely keep myself above water. . . . when the two Islanders saw me, now supporting myself by a floating oar, and made for me. The poor fellows tried to haul me into the boat, but their strength failed them. At last, taking hold of my clothes in their teeth, they fortunately succeeded. We then stood out to sea as night set in, and a darker one I never saw. The Owyhees, overcome with wet and cold, began to lose hope, and their fortitude forsook them.[6]

The boat made it to shore eventually, but not before one of the Kanakas died.

The dead man was buried by six Kanaka comrades according to their tribal customs. Each before leaving the ship had taken an offering of biscuit, pork or tobacco. They put the biscuit under the arm of the deceased, the pork under the chin and the tobacco under the testicles or genital organs. Then they put the body in the grave and after covering it with sand and gravel they formed a double line, with their faces turned eastwards. One officiating as a priest went to fetch water in his hat and having sprinkled the two rows of Islanders, began a prayer to which the others responded. Then they rose and departed and made their way towards the ship without looking back.[7]

This unnamed Kanaka was the first, but far from last, to lose his life in the treacherous coastal waters of the Pacific Northwest.

Fate was unkind to many of the others as well. While one group of Kanakas helped to build the trading post near the mouth of the Columbia in what is now Oregon, the other contingent went with the *Tonquin* on its first upcoast trading voyage. At an anchorage on Vancouver Island's west coast, Captain Thorn offended a local native chief. The next day the Indians returned, as if to trade, but suddenly brandished knives and massacred the crew. An Indian interpreter survived to tell the grim tale of how one wounded crew member lived long enough to set fire to the ship's powder magazine and blow up the vessel with scores of Indians on board. All the Kanakas perished.

❊ ❊ ❊

At Astoria, the gruelling work of hacking a site out of virgin bush and building the fort went forward. According to one account, after two months of cutting and blasting trees and stumps, they had cleared scarcely an acre of ground.

> In the meantime three of our men were killed by the natives, two more wounded by the falling of trees, and one had his hand blown off by gunpowder. . . . The people suffered greatly from the humidity of the climate. The Sandwich Islanders, used to a dry, pure atmosphere, sank under its influence; damp fogs and sleet were frequent . . . and all this time we were without tents or shelter. Add to this the bad quality of our food. . . . so that one-half of the party, on an average, were constantly on the sick list.[8]

Later, they took to fishing and hunting, and an eyewitness gives quite a different impression: "Those who adapted themselves best to our new diet were the Islanders, who thought the fish and the venison delicious."[9]

To accompany and look after the interests of this first group of Kanaka contract labourers, King Kamehameha had appointed a royal observer of high rank named Naukane. He was part of the extended family from the Big Island of Hawaii that had taken power with Kamehameha in 1810, and he later claimed to have witnessed Captain Cook's death. Because of his resemblance to one of the *Tonquin*'s white crew, he was dubbed John Coxe and retained this name throughout his colourful career as Hawaii's first "soldier of fortune."

Coxe's adventures began in July, the same month the fort was completed. The intrepid surveyor and mapmaker David Thompson and a small party from the rival North West Company appeared at Astoria. Intending to establish their own claim to an outlet on the Pacific, they had made the long journey across the Rockies and down the Columbia. The Astor men wined and dined them. Thompson rested a week before heading back up the river, but not before the Americans gave him one of our Sandwich Islanders, a bold and trustworthy fellow named Cox, for one of his men, a Canadian, called Boulard. Boulard had the advantage of being long in the Indian country, and had picked up a few words of the language on his way down. Cox, again, was looked upon by Mr. Thompson as a prodigy of wit and humor, so that those respectively acceptable qualities led to the exchange.[10]

Released from his contract (and apparently ignoring his obligations to the Hawaiian king), Coxe became a loyal North West Company employee and accompanied Thompson by canoe and portage halfway across the continent to the company's supply depot and central meeting place at Fort William on Lake Superior (now Thunder Bay, Ontario), which they reached in July 1812. Three days later a ship arrived with news that the United States had declared war on Britain.

The North West Company decided to send a party to England, outfit a ship, and send it halfway around the world to seize Astoria. Coxe went along, by way of Montreal, in part to act as pilot because he was familiar with the Columbia River bar. After a series of exciting twists and turns—he was briefly shanghaied in Portsmouth, England, and nearly killed by an exploding shipboard cannon—he returned to Astoria in late 1813 on board H.M.S. *Racoon,* only to learn that an overland party from the North West Company had peacefully negotiated the surrender (and purchase) of Astoria.

Coxe stayed on at the renamed Fort George with what remained of the original group of Kanakas (and twenty-six others who had arrived on the *Beaver* in May 1812) until August 1814, when he returned to Hawaii.

But the North West Company had been favourably impressed by the Kanakas and continued to recruit them for work at Fort George and its growing network of interior

John Coxe.
Paul Kane.

trading posts. There they occupied the lowest rung on the social ladder. The British led the operations and kept the books. The French Canadians— often these were Métis and were simply referred to as Canadians—handled the boats and trapped. The Kanakas did the most menial jobs and were only occasionally allowed to trap.

Kanakas were also valued as soldiers. Ross Cox, a North West Company clerk, wrote that they were

> not wanting in courage, particularly against the Indians, for whom they entertain a very cordial contempt, and if they were let loose against them, they rush upon them like tigers. The principal purpose for which they were useful on the Columbia was as an array of numbers in view of natives especially in the frequent voyages up and down the communications. [11]

During one expedition, a canoe party from Fort George was forced into a showdown with a vastly superior force of Indians. The party's leader, James Keith, "addressed the Sandwich Islanders, and asked them, would they fight the bad people who had attempted to rob us, in case it was necessary? Their answer was laconic: 'Missi Keith, we kill every man you bid us.' "[12]

Another time, Ross Cox was threatened by Indian attack at Fort Okanogan (on the Upper Columbia in what is now Washington State), where half of his men were Kanakas:

> My two Canadians were out hunting at the period of the robbery; and the whole of my household troops merely consisted of Bonaparte! Washington!! and Cesar!!! (The individuals bearing these formidable names were merely three unsophisticated natives of the Sandwich Islands.) Great names, you will say; but I must confess, that much as I think of the two great moderns, and highly as I respect the memory of the immortal Julius, among these thieving scoundrels "a rose, by any other name, would smell as sweet." The snow is between two and three feet deep, and my trio of Owhyee generals find a sensible difference between such hyperborean weather and the pleasing sun-shine of their own tropical paradise. Poor fellows! They are not adapted for these latitudes, and I heartily wish they were at home in their own sweet islands, and sporting in the "blue summer ocean" that surrounds them. [13]

A lot of brute manual labour was needed at Fort George. The fort could not rely entirely on food supplies brought in by ship, and had to plant crops to feed itself. By 1817, two hundred acres of land had been cleared for agriculture. In 1818 the post had around fifty men, more than half of them Kanakas. That same year, the North West Company established Fort Walla Walla far in the interior. Among its employees were twenty-five Canadians (mainly men of mixed Indian-white parentage born in Upper Canada), thirty-eight Iroquois Indians and thirty-two Kanakas. The Iroquois plotted against the fort's leader, Donald Mackenzie, and attacked him one night, but he was saved by ". . . some of the Canadians and faithful Owhyhees. . . ."[14] In 1820 three of these Kanakas were murdered while hunting beaver among the Snake Indians, and the river where this occurred was subsequently named the Owyhee.

By the early 1820s, the practice of recruiting Kanakas for work on the Northwest Coast was firmly established. By this time, too, the North West Company had a firm foothold in the Columbia region. It had long been engaged, however, in fierce (and at times violent) competition throughout much of the north and west with the rival Hudson's Bay Company. In 1821 the British government virtually forced the two firms to merge. Many of the North West personnel were absorbed into what continued to be called the Hudson's Bay Company (HBC). For the Kanakas, the merger led to an improvement in the terms of service and a great expansion of opportunities for employment. It was, therefore, in service to the Hudson's Bay Company that most of the Kanakas who eventually settled in British Columbia and the Pacific Northwest were recruited and brought to North America.

3
A Boisterous Little Community

K anakas played a major role in the growth of the Hudson's Bay Company in the west. When the North West Company merged with the HBC, its ninety-seven trading posts were added to the HBC's seventy-six. This resulted in considerable duplication of facilities. The HBC's resident governor in North America, George Simpson, reorganized the continent-spanning network to make it more efficient and profitable. In many parts of what is now northern and western Canada posts were closed and employees laid off. In the relatively unexploited fur territory of the Columbia River, however, and in the coastal region to the north, the company's trade system was soon expanded dramatically. Kanakas who had worked for the North West Company were transferred to the HBC, and growth created a demand for additional Kanaka labourers.

One of Simpson's major changes was to establish a new headquarters and depot for the Columbia region. This enormous territory included not only the Columbia Valley and the valleys of such major tributaries as the Snake and Willamette rivers, but the Puget Sound area and much of what is now British Columbia. The new post, Fort Vancouver, was nearly one hundred miles up from the mouth of the Columbia on a defensible plateau on the river's north shore. Compared with Fort George, which remained in operation as a minor trading post, Fort Vancouver enjoyed two advantages. The better climate and large area of fertile soil gave it the potential to feed not only the fort itself, but also the remote inland and upcoast posts and the company ships that were such a vital link in the trading network. (Eventually, Fort Vancouver produced surpluses of food that were exported to Hawaii and to the Russian posts in Alaska.) A second advantage was that Fort

Vancouver was on the north bank of the Columbia. In 1818 Britain and the United States had agreed to joint occupancy of the Oregon Country. As American settlers pushed westward in increasing numbers, the Columbia River—roughly forty-six degrees north latitude—was thought likely to become the eventual boundary between British and American territory.

Fort Vancouver, which was officially inaugurated by Simpson in March 1825, grew rapidly into a permanent, self-sustaining settlement of planked houses and sheds surrounding the central log stockade. It also became the home base for what was probably the largest single group of Hawaiians ever to congregate outside their native Islands.

Although it was far upriver, Fort Vancouver could be reached by deep-draught sea-going ships, which was essential to its unique role as a depot. Trade goods were sent from Fort Vancouver to smaller posts, most of which were manned only by one or two officers and a small contingent of labourers (called servants by the HBC). Furs traded by the Indians at each post, or trapped by the HBC employees themselves, were dispatched to Fort Vancouver by regularly scheduled canoe, boat, and horse brigades, loaded onto company ships, and transported to Europe. Much of the labour at each stage in this arduous process was performed by Kanakas.

The recruitment of Kanakas expanded with the growing west coast fur trade. The HBC soon improved the inducements for young men to sign up, usually for an initial three-year stint. Whereas the North West Company had paid room, board, clothing, and merchandise, the HBC at first offered them room, board, and a wage of ten pounds a year. (When agriculture and fishing came into full production at Fort Vancouver, the standard weekly ration per man was twenty-one pounds of salmon and a bushel of potatoes.) At these wages, they were considered a bargain, esteemed as better workers than "half-breeds" or Indians and cheaper to hire than French Canadians.

As Astor's men and the North West Company had learned, the Kanakas were loyal employees with a willingness to fight the Indians. Governor Simpson noted that "a few Sandwich Islanders mixed among the Canadians and Europeans can be usefully employed here as guards and for common drudgery about the establishments." He considered them unfit for long sea voyages—a generation of whaling captains disagreed—but felt "they can be depended upon in cases of danger from the natives."[1] He particularly praised the role of a half dozen Hawaiians during a threatened Indian attack in 1829 on the Umpqua River.

Kanakas quickly became a major part of the labour force at Fort

Vancouver. Eventually they constituted the largest single ethnic group. In 1830–31—the HBC operated on a calendar of "Outfit" years, which ran from June 1 to the following May 31—there were 16 Hawaiians working at Fort Vancouver (not including those at the smaller posts) or 15 percent of the 104 men employed at the time. But the big expansion was yet to come. In 1840 the Hawaiian governor Kekuanoao gave the HBC's Honolulu agent permission to "take 60 Hawaiians for the Company's service on the Columbia River for a period of 3 years, to be returned at the end of said term on penalty of $20 each, excepting only in the event of death."[2] In 1842 Simpson decided the company had too many Kanakas and that no more should be hired, but Fort Vancouver's Chief Factor John McLoughlin disagreed and requested an additional 50 to replace retiring French Canadians and employees who had died.

There was a continual turnover of men. HBC ships plied the route between Hawaii and the Columbia on average twice a year. Of some 310 Kanakas who served with the Hudson's Bay Company in 1842–43 or later, at least 91 took the opportunity to return home following the expiration of their contracts. (Of those, at least 26 eventually returned to HBC service.) By comparison, 49 men died while in HBC service and 119 stayed in North America beyond their years with the company. (For 51 others there is too little information to draw a conclusion about how they ended their relationship with the HBC and what became of them.)[3]

By 1843–44 the number of Kanakas based at Fort Vancouver had increased to 57, or 43 percent of the 134 men then employed there, and this does not include those working elsewhere in the Columbia District. Kanaka employment peaked around 1845–46, when 119 Kanakas worked at Fort Vancouver and nearby Cowlitz Farm. This represented over 50 percent of the total roster of servants. That year, a total of 207 Kanakas worked at the forts, farms, and on the coastal ships of the HBC from California to the panhandle of Alaska.[4]

Nearly all of these Hawaiian employees were young men—most entered service in their early to mid-twenties—from the class of commoners. They were listed on the HBC books as "labourers" or "midmen" (the middle position in a canoe), a distinction that meant little. All company servants were expected to pitch in at any task that needed doing, be it guard duty at the forts, farm labour, maintenance work, or any of the tasks associated with paddling or portaging canoes and cleaning, drying, sorting, and baling furs. In practice, some Kanakas specialized in particular tasks and worked as shepherds, sawyers, cooks, coopers, and woodcutters or stokers on steamships. Seldom, however, did they receive more than a small bonus (or gratuity) for such expertise, or for particularly loyal service as cooks and household help for company officers. And none ever rose above the rank of servant to clerk or officer.[5] As general labourers, the two main jobs done by Kanakas at Fort Vancouver were sawmilling and farming.

Stands of fine timber cloaked the hills and mountains of the entire Northwest Coast. The HBC found that construction in the Sandwich Islands provided an excellent market for lumber, and the company seldom overlooked a chance to supplement its fur earnings with other commerce. In 1828 it established a water-powered sawmill about five miles upstream from Fort Vancouver and staffed it with an eight-man crew of Kanakas. They were paid seventeen pounds per year, plus board, which consisted mainly of smoked salmon and sea biscuit. In 1830, 200,000 feet of lumber were shipped to Hawaii.

The Kanakas proved to be excellent mill workers. According to one historian, envy on the part of white employees forced the HBC to cut their wages back to ten pounds, but this is not supported by the HBC employment records. From the late 1830s through the 1850s, Kanakas earned exactly the same wages as whites, half-breeds or Iroquois engaged in similar work for similar lengths of service. In 1844–45 the Willamette Valley sawmill employed eighteen labourers, fifteen of them Kanakas. They earned either seventeen or twenty-seven pounds annually, depending on their years of service, as did their non-Kanaka co-workers.

In fact, the HBC had a policy of paying more for newcomers to the service than to those who had been with the company for three years or more. Officers took pride in getting the men drunk when it was time to renew their contracts. At Fort Langley, Archibald McDonald wrote about a debauch that went on for three days,

> after which we tried the people's disposition to renew their contracts for this place in which I am happy to say we have succeeded to our full expectations—as many as we require are engaged for two & some for three years, and several of them at reduced wages . . .[6]

Fort Vancouver's rapidly expanding agricultural holdings also provided work for Kanaka hands. Between 1829 and 1841, the area of land under cultivation increased tenfold to around twelve hundred acres, and thousands more had been cleared for pasture. There was a grist mill to grind wheat, oats, and barley. Hawaii became a major market for flour, as well as lumber and fish. Also important were fruit, peas, root crops, and squash. The fort's livestock holdings included cattle, horses, pigs, sheep, goats, chickens, turkeys, and pigeons. In 1838, twenty-three of the fort's seventy-four servants were employed in farm work. American visitors in 1841 reported seeing farming on a "stupendous scale," with an abundance of crops and "vast quantities of butter and cheese."[7] By 1846, at Fort Vancouver's peak, the farmland stretched for twenty-five miles along the river and reached inland for ten. A visitor in 1848 watched Indians, Kanakas, and Scots shear fifteen to twenty thousand head of sheep.

Fort Vancouver was the ultimate company town; the HBC was employer, landlord, shopkeeper, creditor, and only provider of transportation or communications home. Life for the Kanakas at Fort Vancouver—as for all HBC servants—consisted of dawn-to-dusk drudgery under rigid, military-style discipline. There was a six-day work week, with only Sundays off. However grim this may sound by modern standards, the Kanakas at the fort enjoyed greater privacy and personal freedom than most men (of any race or rank) who worked on nineteenth-century sailing ships.

Unlike the company's officers and their families, servants were housed outside the stockade in the "Kanaka Village," a "boisterous little community . . . where the Company's employees of lower rank—Iroquois, Scottish, Hawaiian, French and Métis—lived with their Indian wives and fami-

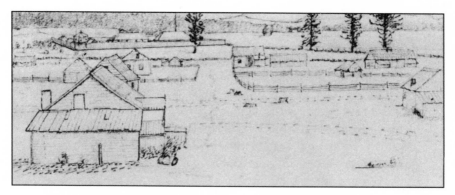

The Kanaka village on the west side of Fort Vancouver, 1851.
George Gibbs.

lies."[8] In fact, the community was not so little. At its peak, it consisted of around 535 men, 254 Indian women, and 301 children. There were only thirty to fifty small wooden houses, so families were crowded together in shared accommodations. The houses were neither planned nor financed by the company, but left to the individual servants to build, and most had only one or two rooms, some papered on the inside, others plastered with clay.

Reverend Herbert Beaver, the fort's chaplain from 1836 to 1838, described the Kanakas' position at Fort Vancouver as "little better than slavery." They were "subject to all the imperious treatment which their employers may think fit to lay on them, whether by flogging, imprisonment or otherwise, without a possibility of obtaining redress."[9] Beaver recounted the fate of one "poor Sandwich Islander" who was flogged and put in irons, which were not removed for over five months.[10] As for remuneration, he lamented that the Kanakas

> before embarkation in their own country, received a small advance of money, part of which their chiefs seize as a bonus for permitting them to have it. . . . The remainder is usually squandered; so that when they arrive in a colder climate they are destitute of adequate clothing, the supply of which generally consumed the whole of their wages for the first year. Nor are they afterwards able to save much of these, for all their necessaries are charged at the rate of 100 percent . . .[11]

This sounds somewhat exaggerated. In fact, the HBC's Honolulu agency office regularly advanced twenty to seventy dollars to each Kanaka at the beginning of his contract period.

Reverend Beaver was especially concerned about the Kanakas' moral and spiritual life. He noted that the Kanakas

> who have been more than ten or twelve years in the service, are totally uninstructed [in religion]; while those who have entered it at later periods have been, for the most part, instructed by the missionaries in their native land previous to leaving it, and many of them can read in their own language. But, from their almost entire ignorance of any other they are necessarily without instruction, and thus the little Christianity, which they brought with them, becomes speedily forgotten and lost, and then former good but unstable, principles are quickly undermined by the inroads of surrounding corruptions. Removed from

Fort Vancouver on the Columbia River, 1840s.
(HBCA/PAM/Kashnor/ P-133/N5318)

the eye of their Pastors, these half-reclaimed savages have in several cases, reverted to certain abominable practices of their idolatrous times.[12]

The drinking habits of Kanakas were also of concern to missionaries who years later visited Hawaiian miners in the California Gold Rush. One of them, writing in the Honolulu missionary journal, *The Friend,* expressed particular outrage upon finding an educated American lawyer selling liquor to Kanakas. The words he chooses tell as much about the casual racism of the times as it does about Kanaka behaviour:

The idea that a man educated in Christian America, should descend so low as *to peddle rum to Kanakas,* was one degree of degradation lower than we had imagined a man could go. It reminded us of the doggerel, a little varied:

"I'd sooner black my visage o'er
And put de shine on boot and shoe,
Than stand within a rum-shop door
And tempt kanakas to my store."[13]

In part to counteract excessive drunkenness, gambling, fighting, and other "corruptions" among the Kanaka half of his work force, Chief Factor McLoughlin asked the HBC's Honolulu agent "to search out a trusty educated Hawaiian of good character to read the scriptures and assemble his people for public worship."[14] William R. Kaulehelehe, who became better known as Kanaka William, arrived in June 1845 with his wife Mary S. Kaai to a largely hostile reception from the Hawaiian community. Part of his flock feared that the new chaplain intended to force them to observe the Sabbath, which was their only free day for gardening, carpentry, and horseback riding. Others, however, apparently hoped he would act as an agent of the Hawaiian king, much as John Coxe (Naukane) had been delegated to do at Astoria, and would look after and defend their interests. Kanaka William wrote:

> the Hawaiians have repeatedly and daily asked me to see about their trouble of being repeatedly abused by the white people without any cause. They thought I had come as an officer to settle their difficulties. I said no, I did not come to do those things. I had no instructions from the king and ministers of the government of Hawaii to do those things. All that I have come for was the word of God and school.[15]

Given the hostility, Kanaka William, unlike the other Hawaiians, was allowed to live within the stockade, where his church came to be known as the Owhyhee Church. He had some success with his preaching, reporting ". . . a little order on Sundays now, not like former times when there was much disturbance."[16] He had wanted to establish a school, but found the workday too long and the nights too short for a night school. Nevertheless, in the HBC employment records of the 1850s he is listed not as a minister, but as a teacher. And his wage of fifty pounds in 1854–55 was much higher than the twenty pounds or so earned by most Kanaka labourers. In 1848 his congregation ranged from twenty to forty each Sunday, but he still had trouble keeping down the consumption of alcohol. "The Hawaiians," a visitor to Fort Vancouver noted, "prove their tendency to become beastly drunkards. They drink without mercy, buy it on Saturday and have Sabbath to get sober in so as to work on Monday. Some Americans bring it over [across the river] and sell it clandestinely just below the fort to all classes."[17]

As for Kanaka morality, it does not seem to have differed from that of whites or Canadian Métis. At least eight Kanaka men formally married Indian women between 1838 and 1842 at Fort Vancouver. Many had their children baptized—seven in July and August of 1838 alone—even when these were the offspring of unsanctified marriages to Indian women "in the manner of the country." In fact, liaisons between fur trade employees and native Indians were actively encouraged by the company. Judging by the experience of Kanaka-Indian families in later British Columbia, many of the common-law marriages were solid, lifetime commitments.

Fort Vancouver may have resembled a military camp in its organization and discipline. (A United States Army camp later arose on the site.) For many Kanakas, though, it was the only home they knew for decades. And if living and working conditions there seem harsh by modern standards, they must have been acceptable by the yardsticks of the time and compared to opportunities at home in Hawaii. The Kanaka Village may have been a rough-and-tumble frontier settlement, but for a few years Fort Vancouver was much the largest, busiest, and most cosmopolitan settlement on the Pacific coast north of Spanish California.

❊ ❊ ❊

As for its Kanakas, aside from William Kaulehelehe, the most notable was old John Coxe (Naukane), the former royal observer at Astoria in 1811, who had initially returned to the Islands to what a Hawaiian historian called "a comfortable life as a lesser chief in Prince Liholiho's court."[18] King Kamehameha I died in 1819, and Liholiho ascended the throne as Kamehameha II. In 1823 the king sailed to England to seek an alliance with the British. Naukane was part of the retinue because of his high rank and familiarity with western ways. In England, most of the royal party came down with measles and, though Naukane survived, the king and queen both died. The *Times* (of London) reported their illnesses in great detail, right up until the king's "vital spark had fled."[19] Their bodies were returned to Honolulu in sealed, leaded coffins. A large sum of the late king's money was missing, and Naukane and the others in the king's court were disgraced and even under suspicion. It is likely that, for his own health, he had to make himself scarce.

By 1827, at any rate, Naukane had returned to the Northwest Coast fur trade and to his identity as John Coxe. According to one account, he worked only a few years at Fort Vancouver, then retired and was given a plot of land two miles below the fort. When pig-keeping expanded, he came out of retirement to become the fort's swineherd, grazing his pigs on the plain between the fort and the river, which was later called Coxe's Plain.

Coxe worked at the fort as a pigherd as late as 1842–43, when, according to the HBC records, he was sixty-two years old. He was still making purchases from the company stores in 1845–46. He posed for artist Paul Kane in 1847. A Protestant cleric who stopped at Fort Vancouver in 1848 went to visit the Hawaiian Cox, who saw Captain Cook murdered. He [was] about 82 years of age. He [had] traveled some, to Eng[land], Am[erica] etc. [Coxe] does not wish to go to the Islands, does not care to attend meeting.[20]

A visitor in 1849 talked to an "old Kanaka" who had been on the *Tonquin* and had travelled to England. Still another recalled talking to an old Kanaka "who used to tell us with a great deal of pride of the part he took in the despatching of Captain Cook and of his having participated in the subsequent feast."[21] And, most intriguing of all, there was a "Captain Coxe," who led the Hawaiians at Kanaka Dam in 1850 during the California Gold Rush (see Chapter 7).

Coxe (or Naukane) appears to have had a son, nephew, or other younger relative, referred to in HBC records as Naukanna, who followed him into Hudson's Bay Company service, starting at Fort Vancouver in 1845–46. Under the name William Naukana, he became prominent among the Kanakas who settled much later in British Columbia's Gulf Islands (see Chapters 14 and 15).

Coxe, the one-time "paragon of wit and humour," must have been quite a storyteller. If his age in the HBC employment records (sixty-two years in 1842–43) is correct, he was not yet born when Captain Cook was killed, and could not have partaken of the feast, if such there was. (Some Kanakas vehemently denied that their ancestors ever practised cannibalism. See Chapter 4 for the protests of Richard Dana's friend Bingham.) In any case, the story of his eating Captain Cook has been passed down to become part of local lore on Salt Spring Island, B.C. One of many apocryphal tales in Bea Hamilton's history of Salt Spring is of Kea, a timid Kanaka who hid every time a white schoolteacher named Cooke came around. Kea assumed that Cooke was a descendant of the great explorer. Once, inadvertently finding himself face to face with the teacher, "the Kanaka shrank back jabbering, 'No-no-be angry— I no kill your grandfather and no eat him!' "[22]

If Coxe was indeed too young to have witnessed Captain Cook's death, he might well have been young enough to leave Fort Vancouver at the time of the California Gold Rush—as many Kanakas did—and lead the group of prospectors at Kanaka Dam. This would be a more fitting conclusion to his career as a soldier of fortune than tending pigs.

4

Outlaws and Beachcombers of the Pacific

M ost Kanakas who eventually settled on the Northwest Coast came to North America with the Hudson's Bay Company. But the HBC was not the only organized trading company that brought Kanakas to the coast. Joint British-American occupancy of the Columbia region, agreed to in 1818, allowed for competition from the United States. In 1834 Nathaniel J. Wyeth, an American, came overland from St. Louis to establish a combined fur trading, salmon, and lumber shipping company in the area. His supply ship, the *May Dacre,* arrived at Fort Vancouver with "twenty Sandwich Islanders and two Coopers two Smiths and a Clerk" mainly to work at Fort Hall, far up the Snake River in what is now Idaho.[1]

This contingent of Kanakas proved to be anything but loyal or docile. One group of thirteen quickly deserted, taking with them some trade goods and twelve horses. Indians soon reported that some of them had stolen native-owned horses and shot a chief. In February 1835 Wyeth wrote of the Hawaiians that

> ten took the trail over the Blue—one was drowned in crossing some ford one froze in the upper country—that the residue rafted on the Snake river one more died somehow about the falls [and] that seven are gone down to Vancouver.[2]

At Fort Vancouver Wyeth found the survivors, who had been chastened by their escapade, and decided not to treat them harshly. Most agreed to go back to work, but Wyeth's venture ultimately failed. In 1837 he was forced to break up his company, sell his property to the HBC, and pay the rival

Sutter's Fort, New Helvetia (Sacramento), 1847.
(California State Library, Sacramento)

company to provide passage for nine of his Kanakas back to Hawaii. At least three of Wyeth's men apparently stayed to work for the HBC.

Kanakas also came to California in 1839 under contract to Captain John Sutter, a quixotic German-Swiss would-be empire builder. Hoping to make his fortune in what was still Mexico, he bought an abandoned ship in Honolulu, crewed it with eight Hawaiian men and two women and landed at Yerba Buena, now San Francisco. With three white followers, and propelled by Kanaka oarsmen, the motley little group went up the Sacramento River in small boats and established the colony of New Helvetia at what would become the California state capital, Sacramento.

Sutter received a large land grant from the Mexican government and became a Mexican citizen and official. Relying mainly on his Kanakas, he built a fort, a mill, and a tannery, and cleared land for farming. Kanakas also built the first frame houses in Sacramento and fought for Sutter in skirmishes with the local Indians. Soon his Kanaka boatmen were a regular sight on shopping trips down to Yerba Buena and the ranches around what is now San Francisco Bay.

Sutter offended Mexican (Catholic) sensibilities by living in "open concubinage" with the Kanaka women. He later also kept a "harem" of young Indian girls. He picked the losing side in an insurrection in 1845 against the Mexican governor and found himself imprisoned for a time, along with several of his Kanaka followers. Then he sided with the Americans in 1846 when they annexed California. Just when Sutter's situation was improving, gold was discovered on his property in 1848. He tried to keep it a secret, but American squatters soon overran his land and stole his cattle and sheep. Many of his workers left him to seek their own fortunes in gold mining.

Sutter's Kanakas remained loyal the longest. One of them, Kanaka Harry, was the trusted major-domo of his Hock Farm. Harry's brother, not identified by name, was drowned in 1848 while serving on Sutter's river boat. Another, nicknamed Maintop, was helmsman on the same boat. But after Sutter left California in 1851, many of the Kanakas also joined the gold rush. Later, they established several small colonies in California, notably one at Verona on the Sacramento, where they intermarried with local Indians and fished for salmon.

One of Sutter's Kanakas was named Ione (John) Keaala o Kaaina (also known as John Kelly). He was the grandson of Tianna (or Ka-i'ana), the chief who left the Islands in 1787 and visited Nootka with Captain William Douglas. Keaala's grandmother (Tianna's wife) was from the Hawaiian royal family. After leaving Sutter's employ, Keaala married a Maidu Indian woman named Mele and accompanied her and her people when the United States government forced them onto a reservation. Resenting this confinement, Keaala, a literate and well-connected man, wrote a letter to the king of Hawaii protesting his treatment and claiming his rights as a Hawaiian subject. This eventually led to the release of him and his family.

Keaala worked for many years on the Sacramento river boats. On one trip, United States Army General John Bidwell, who was also a major landowner in northern California, was knocked overboard. Keaala dove in and saved Bidwell from drowning, earning him the officer's lifelong gratitude. Keaala's daughter, best known by her later married name Mary Azbill, travelled to meet the Hawaiian royal family when they visited the United States in 1887. Largely due to her royal blood—she chanted her family's genealogy to King Kalakaua in his private railway car—she was made a lady-in-waiting to Princess Liliuokalani. In 1891 she accompanied the king's body when it was returned to Hawaii on a U.S. Navy cruiser after his death in San Francisco. Mary eventually settled in the California town of Chico, where General Bidwell's family had a ranch. She worked for them, as well as at the Indian school they helped to support.

Another source of employment for Islanders in the Northwest was the American Protestant clerics who established missions among the Cayuse and Nez Percé Indians. The missionaries arrived with no labour force of

Mary Azbill (Mele Kainuha Keaala Azbill), 1846–1932.
(Special Collections, Meriam Library, Calif. State Univ., Chico & Dorothy Hill)

their own and soon found the local Indian workers to be un-reliable. A number of Kanakas were seconded by the HBC to work temporarily for these missions. By the 1840s small groups of Kanakas, some re-cruited directly from Honolulu, were being employed to build the missions and work on mission farms. Here again, they were particularly valued for their loyalty during conflicts with the Indians. In one case, a Kanaka stepped in to save the life of Reverend Henry H. Spalding during a bitter argument with an Indian.

❈   ❈   ❈

As settlers flooded into the Willamette Valley of Oregon, Kanakas were employed in the private economy. In 1846 five Kanakas worked for an American merchant, A. E. Wilson, in his sawmill at Astoria. Wilson con-tracted directly for labourers with the Hawaiian king at the rate of five dollars per month plus board (salmon and potatoes). Each also received a twenty-one-dollar advance before leaving the Islands. By comparison, white lumbermill workers were receiving twenty dollars per month. Mill-ing could be dangerous work. A local paper reported an accident in which ". . . a Sandwich Islander came very near having his leg amputated by . . . a saw."[3]

The largest number of Kanakas left their homeland not in service to the HBC, Sutter, or missionaries, but as crew members on board whaling and merchant ships. Many of these men settled or worked for extended periods on the west coast of North America. In 1847 the forty resident Kanakas composed nearly ten percent of the population of San Francisco, where most of them worked as boatmen on San Francisco Bay or as steve-dores. (See Chapter 13 for the story of the Browne family.)

The whalers came mainly from New England ports. The first American whaling ships, the *Balaena* of New Bedford and the *Equator* from Nantucket, anchored at Kealakekua Bay in September 1819 and hired Kanakas as crewmen. In the ensuing decades, Kanakas formed a large part of ship's crews on all the oceans. As R. C. Wyllie of the Honolulu missionary newspaper *The Friend* wrote in 1844,

> I have never met any captain of a vessel who did not speak highly of the native seamen whom he had employed. They are eminently subordinate, docile, good natured and trustworthy; and with proper training they become good efficient seamen. Their extraordinary expertness in swimming renders them of great use where boats are employed in surfs. Mr. Dundas ... who took over to San Blas the Hawaiian government schooner *Hooikaika* ... assured me that but for his native crew, several lives, in Mazatlan, would have been lost from the upsetting of boats in the surf there. And he spoke in very high terms of the general conduct of the men while at sea.[4]

A dissenting judgement was provided by James Douglas when he was chief factor at Fort Victoria in 1850. He reported that,

> The barque *Cowlitz* from England arrived here a few days ago.... Nearly all the seamen on board ran from her at the Sandwich Islands from whence she came on with Sandwich Islanders who made a shift to get here but cannot be trusted on a coasting voyage.[5]

The North Pacific whale fishery expanded rapidly. As early as 1823 forty whaling vessels were counted in the port of Honolulu. A history of west coast whaling notes:

> A "mixed crew" was no oddity by 1830 ... crewlists now included .... the ubiquitous Kanakas.... It was no fiction that Herman Melville chose for his three boatsteerers of the *Pequod* a Yankee, an American Indian, and a Pacific Islander. By the time *Moby-Dick* appeared in 1851, that sort of interracial mix was virtually always the case in fact. ... Had the Sandwich Islands been inaccessible ... the development of the whaling business in the North Pacific must have been very differently organized.[6]

The numbers of Kanakas recruited grew to staggering proportions. There are widely conflicting estimates and statistics, in part because the official records did not account for those recruited and leaving informally or illegally, but there is no mistaking the scale of this exodus. In 1841 HBC Governor Simpson, on a visit to Hawaii, reported that

> about a thousand males in the very prime of life are estimated annually to leave the islands, some going to California, others to the Columbia, and many on long and dangerous voyages, particularly in whaling vessels, while a considerable portion of them are said to be permanently lost to their country, either dying during their engagements, or settling in other parts of the world.[7]

A more precise reckoning for the one-and-a-half-year period from January 1, 1843 to June 1, 1844 shows that 275 Hawaiian men signed on to foreign flag ships, including 111 on whalers. (There were also some Hawaiian-built and -registered whaling ships.) The rest joined merchant ships en route to such places as China, Kamchatka, Valparaiso, and Mazatlan. In 1846 Hawaii's minister of the interior reported that 651 Islanders had left on foreign ships in the previous year. Another source estimated that 2000 left in the three-year period from 1845 to 1847.

Many left their ships and stayed in foreign ports. A visitor to Acapulco in 1846 encountered about 15 Kanaka seamen, some of whom had served in the Mexican navy. At other times, there were said to be 500 at Papeete, Tahiti, and 50 at Paita, Peru. Hawaii's interior minister proclaimed: "There is no port in this ocean untrodden by Hawaiians; and they are also in Nantucket, New Bedford, Sag Harbor, New London and other places in the United States."[8]

Of those who went to sea, some perished in shipwrecks. In November 1842 the American whaler *Holder Borden* was lost, but its crew, including five Kanakas, built a small boat from the wreckage and survived. Those on the whaler *Baltic,* which was wrecked off Kamchatka in 1844, were not so lucky. Three Kanakas died. Some seamen died from mistreatment aboard ships, including one case of a Kanaka on a British ship that was investigated by an English court. But in other cases the outcome was happier. In 1854 the whaler *Canton* was lost and the survivors reached an island without water or vegetation. They were saved because, according to the captain, ". . . by the assistance of an expert Kanaka swimmer [some of the crew] were enabled to communicate through the rough seas with the wreck, from which they saved a quantity of bread and other provisions."[9]

Pirate attack was also a danger, as were acts of war. During the American Civil War the Confederate raider *Shenandoah* attacked unarmed Union whaling ships in the north Pacific and captured or burned them, after giving their crews the choice of joining the *Shenandoah* or being marooned. In 1865 around fifty Kanaka crewmen were so captured and returned to the Islands by the ship's captain, who reported that he was "rather partial to Hawaiians."[10]

Even before this exodus of young seamen, diseases introduced by Europeans and Americans (smallpox, measles, and venereal diseases) had ravaged the native Hawaiian population, reducing it from an estimated 300,000 in 1778 to 134,750 in 1823. Because of this population decline, the additional loss of sailors was a great concern. The Hawaiian government responded by limiting recruitment to the ports of Honolulu (on Oahu) and Lahaina (on Maui), by requiring the consent of each island's governor, and by demanding that the individual Hawaiians present their passports. Vessels violating these rules were subject to a fine of four hundred dollars. In a separate measure, the Hawaiian government levied a tax on Kanakas who were leaving families behind to ensure that they were properly supported. Still, the census of 1849 showed that the native population had continued to decline dramatically, and this was attributed in large part to the "large number of Hawaiian youth who have left on whaleships and never returned."[11] When the California Gold Rush led to even more emigration, the government tried additional measures (see Chapter 7) but nothing seemed to work. By 1860 an astonishing twelve percent of Hawaiian males over the age of eighteen had left the Islands.

Besides whaling, many Kanakas worked on merchant ships that carried goods between pre-gold rush California, Hawaii, and the coasts of Chile and Peru. The most vivid and engaging description of these men and how they lived comes from the pen of Richard Henry Dana Jr., a Harvard man who signed onto an American ship as a common seaman and wrote the remarkable memoir, *Two Years Before the Mast.* One ship he encountered in 1835 at what is now San Diego flew the American flag, but most of the crew were Islanders. Another, at San Pedro, had a mixed crew of Americans, English, Spaniards, Spanish Indians, and Sandwich Islanders.

Dana found his own American crewmates to be a less-than-congenial bunch and soon fell in with "a dozen or twenty" Islanders who had been paid off by their ships and were living on the beach at San Diego and "keeping up a grand carnival." A Russian discovery ship had been there a few years before and built a large oven for baking bread. The Kanakas had taken this over as a bunkhouse, where they lived

> in complete idleness—drinking, playing cards and carousing in every way. They bought a bullock once a week, which kept them in meat, and one of them went up to the town every day to get fruit, liquor, and provisions. . . . There they lived, having a grand time, and caring for nobody.[12]

Their leader, Mannini, "a finely built, active, strong and intelligent fellow. . . . was known all over California." A ship's captain came to hire the men for work, offering fifteen dollars a month and one month's pay in advance. "But it was like throwing pearls before swine," Dana wrote, "or rather, carrying coals to Newcastle. So long as they had money, they would not work for fifty dollars a month, and when their money was gone, they would work for ten."

The captain asked Mannini how he and his men spent their time:

> "Oh, we play cards, get drunk, smoke—do anything we're a mind to."
> "Don't you want to come aboard and work?"
> "*Aole! aole make make makou i ka hana.* Now, got plenty money; no good, work. *Mamule*, money *pau*—all gone. Ah! very good, work!—*maikai, hana hana nui!*"
> "But you'll spend all your money in this way," said the captain.
> "Aye! Me know that. By-'em-by money *pau*—all gone; then Kanaka work plenty."
> This was a hopeless case, and the captain left them, to wait patiently until their money was gone.[13]

Dana stayed four months at San Diego, worked with the Kanakas at a cowhide-curing warehouse and became extremely fond of them. "Their language," he wrote,

> I could only learn, orally, for they had not any books among them, though many of them had been taught to read and write by the mis-

sionaries at home. They spoke a little English, and by a sort of compromise, a mixed language was used on the beach, which could be understood by all.[14]

One of the Kanakas could read, write, and do arithmetic:

His education was as good as that of three-quarters of the Yankees in California, and his manners and principles a good deal better, and he was so quick of apprehension that he might have been taught navigation, and the elements of many of the sciences, with the most perfect ease.

Another, Mr. Bingham, "was the best-hearted old fellow in the world. He must have been over fifty years of age, and had two of his front teeth knocked out, which was done by his parents as a sign of grief at the death of Kamehameha, the great king of the Sandwich Islands."[15]

Then Dana sheds light on the touchy issue of cannibalism:

We used to tell [Mr. Bingham] that he ate Captain Cook and lost his teeth in that way. That was the only thing that ever made him angry. He would always be quite excited at that; and say—"*Aole!*" (no.) "Me no eat Captain Cook! Me pikinini—small—so high—no more! My father see Captain Cook! Me—no!" None of them like to have anything said about Captain Cook, for the sailors all believe that he was eaten, and that, they cannot endure to be taunted with.—"New Zealand Kanaka eat white man;—Sandwich Island Kanaka,—no. Sandwich Island Kanaka *ua like pu na haole*—all 'e same a' you!"[16]

Bingham may have soon left California and returned to Hawaii, for a Kanaka by that name was recruited there by the HBC in August 1837 to serve at Fort Vancouver.

When he discussed the everyday values of his Kanaka friends, Dana waxed downright sentimental:

I would have trusted my life and my fortune in the hands of any one of these people; and certainly had I wished for a favor or act of sacrifice, I would have gone to them all, in turn, before I should have applied to one of my own countrymen on the coast. . . . Their costumes, and manner of treating one another, show a simple, primitive generosity, which is truly delightful; and which is often a reproach to our own people. Whatever one has, they all have. Money, food, clothes, they share with one another; even to the last piece of tobacco to put in their pipes. I once heard old Mr. Bingham say, with the highest indignation to a Yankee trader who was trying to persuade him to keep his money to himself—"No! We no all 'e same a' you! Suppose one got money, all got money. You;—suppose one got money—lock him up in chest.— No good!"—"Kanaka all 'e same a' one!" This principle they carry so far, that none of them will eat anything in the sight of others without offering it all round.[17]

Dana also noted their strange form of singing:

They run on, in a low, guttural, monotonous sort of chant, their lips and tongues seeming hardly to move, and the sounds modulated solely in the throat. There is very little tune to it, and the words, so far as I could learn, are extempore. They sing about persons and things which are around them, and adopt this method when they do not wish to be understood by any but themselves.

Mr. Mannini, the leader, often sang when working among Americans and Englishmen,

and, by the occasional shouts and laughter of the Kanakas, who were at a distance, it was evident that he was singing about the different men that he was at work with. They have great powers of ridicule, and are excellent mimics; many of them discovering and imitating the peculiarities of our own people, before we had seen them ourselves.[18]

The Kanakas at San Diego were always ready for adventure. They showed no fear of rattlesnakes. When one was spotted, they drove it out of a thicket with sticks, killed it with stones, and cut off the rattle. They claimed they had an herb that acted as an antidote to snakebite. While fishing one time, they hooked a shark. The line broke, "but the Kanakas would not let him get off so easily, and sprang directly into the water after him." They grabbed the shark by the tail and dragged him up onto the beach, where he made a lunge at one of the Kanaka's hands. The man had to let go. The shark, thrashing about, made for the water; the Kanakas grabbed him again. Again he got away. "The Kanakas, in high excitement, [were] yelling at the top of their voices; but the shark at last got off, carrying away a hook and line, and not a few severe bruises."[19]

Dana also witnessed the Kanakas' famed swimming abilities. One time, a ship was leaving the harbour when an urgent message for it was brought to the beach. Offered a handful of silver to carry the letter out to the ship, one of the Kanakas

> instantly threw off everything but his duck trowsers, and putting the letter into his hat, swam off after the vessel. Fortunately the wind was very light and the vessel was going slowly, so that, although she was nearly a mile off when he started, he gained on her rapidly. He went through the water leaving a wake like a small steamboat.[20]

When he reached the ship, the captain read the letter and gave the Kanaka a shot of brandy. An hour later he was back at the beach, apparently unfatigued.

Twenty-four years after working with the Kanakas at the crude hide houses of Spanish California, Dana returned to San Diego, by then well on its way to becoming the huge port city it is today. Everything had changed. Of the oven, he found only a few broken bricks and bits of mortar. Of the men, there was not a trace. "Where were they all?" he mused. "Why should I care for them,—poor Kanakas and sailors, the refuse of civilization, the outlaws and beach-combers of the Pacific!"[21]

5

Pitsaws and Sheep Pens

W hile Richard Dana was sharing the seaside life with Kanakas in southern California, other Islanders were well established more than a thousand miles to the north in what would become British Columbia. The HBC had acquired many interior trading posts from the North West Company. A few Kanakas were assigned to Fort St. James in New Caledonia (the northern interior of B.C.) as early as the 1820s (see Chapter 6). Soon the company was pushing north along the coast as well, establishing forts in virgin territory that had been touched only lightly by the ship-borne fur trade.

The key post—and the one most like Fort Vancouver itself, though never on so grand a scale—was Fort Langley on the lower Fraser River. Fort Langley is interesting on several counts. It remained one of the longest-functioning HBC posts on the coast, and has been partially rebuilt as a heritage park and museum. It is one of the forts where Kanakas constituted, at times, a clear majority of all servants. And it engendered a sizeable cluster of Kanaka settlers in the adjacent area.

In 1824, just a few years after the merger of the North West and Hudson's Bay companies, the HBC sent James McMillan and forty-two men to reconnoitre the Lower Fraser. The company hoped to establish a post to tap the fur-trading potential of the Fraser Valley and eastern coast of Vancouver Island and to provide a second terminus on the Pacific for the interior fur trade. Governor Simpson also wanted a second fort with good farmland—both to help provision planned upcoast posts that had poor agricultural conditions and to act as a backup in case some disaster, such as a serious Indian attack, befell Fort Vancouver, or Britain were forced out of the Columbia Valley (which was eventually the case).

This first exploratory party included six Kanakas. One history of Fort Langley describes the Kanakas somewhat condescendingly as "fun-loving Islanders."[1] It is doubtful that the interior route they took—a gruelling one by canoe and portage to Puget Sound which avoided stormy winter sea conditions—was much fun. But the expedition found a site with rich, fertile soil along a river teeming with salmon and sturgeon and surrounded by vast virgin forests. The group surveyed the lower reaches of the Fraser and proclaimed the river to be safe and navigable, leading company officials to view the Fraser—quite falsely—as a viable water route to the rich interior fur country of New Caledonia.

Back at Fort Vancouver plans were made to equip and supply the new post. In 1827 a party to establish Fort Langley was led by McMillan and included three clerks and twenty-one men, among them two Kanakas, Como and Peeohpeeoh, who were to be based at Fort Langley for many years. They came this time by sea with their full outfit on the supply ship *Cadboro,* whose crew included another six Kanakas. Como and Peeohpeeoh were among the longest-serving Kanakas in the fur trade. Both had joined the North West Company before 1820 and had been "inherited" by the HBC. After thirteen or fourteen years at Fort Langley, Como would return to Fort Vancouver, where he worked until his death in 1850 at about the age of fifty-four. Peeohpeeoh stayed in the Fort Langley area for the rest of his life (see Chapter 11).

According to a tale told by HBC trader John Tod, Como was a valued chef, though less than proficient in English:

Travelling on one occasion. . . . I had my cook "Como", nominally a Sandwich Islander, but really, a composite of every human race then existing, with which distraction of lineage his speech corresponded. . . . nevertheless a good, cleanly cook. Looking down the bank, said I, "Como, these are nice salmon in that canoe, but to-day I fancy a bit of young bear," pointing to certain small carcasses on the beach near the canoe, void of heads, tails and feet. "There is no time for braising them with your usual skill—let it be a roast." "Oui! Oui! monsieur," was the reply, and in due course a fine roast appeared on the table. I chewed and chewed, till jaw was weary, then turning to Como, said:

"What on earth is this, Como? How can a young bear be so tough?"
"Bear," replied Como, "he is welly good bow-wow." This ended my
meal . . .[2]

Peeohpeeoh served the HBC even longer than Como—at least until
1853–54—and settled near Fort Langley after that, working as a labourer,
sawyer, and cooper. According to Jason Allard, who grew up at the post,
Peeohpeeoh (also called Peon Peon, Peoh Peoh, and other variations) was
the "foreman" of the Langley Kanakas and a relative of the Hawaiian royal
family. Peeohpeeoh fathered one of the first children to be born at the fort
(a future Mrs. Nahu) and another, Joseph Mayo (or Ma-ayo), whose history
is also interesting (see below and Chapter 11).

From their arrival at the new post, Como and Peeohpeeoh were assigned to such chores as sharpening pitsaws and using them to cut wood for
the stockade and buildings. The Fort Langley journals mention them frequently during the first few months of the fort's construction: "Como &
Peopeoh erecting a saw pit"; "The two Sandwich Islanders sawing"; "Como
& Peopeoh sawing pickets"; "The Two Owyhees are making another
sawpit."[3] Illness occasionally intruded: "Peopeoh is this morning on the
sick list. He complains of acute pain in his loins and violent cholic." A few
days later, "Peo. was blistered yesterday, and feels a good deal relieved in
consequence."[4]

Fort Langley never lived up to its expected potential as a fur-trading
post. As Governor Simpson discovered during his trip down the Fraser to
Langley in 1828—and as he should have known from Simon Fraser's hair-
raising journey in 1808—the deadly rapids (farther upriver than the first
exploratory party had ventured) made the Fraser a nearly suicidal route to
the interior HBC districts of Thompson's River and New Caledonia. Eventually, alternative routes to the interior were found, but they were complex
and arduous, involving several kinds of boats and canoes, as well as pack
trains requiring hundreds of horses.

The fort flourished, however, as a farm and as a fishing and fish-
processing site. It had excellent alluvial soil and a temperate climate. By
1835, seventy to seventy-five acres of land were being tilled. In 1840 thirty
milk cows produced 1,176 pounds of butter. Crops included wheat, barley,
oats, and peas. There was enough to feed Fort Langley and a surplus for
some of the upcoast trading posts. Much of the butter was sold to the Rus-

sians in Alaska. Later, cranberries became an important crop, as they still are in the Fraser Valley. In 1856 the fort exported 469 twenty-four-gallon barrels of berries, all of them to San Francisco. Most of this farm work was performed by Kanaka labourers. The Kanaka work force grew gradually from the original two (Como and Peeohpeeoh) to six in 1837–38, nine in 1841–42, and fifteen in 1848–49, when Hawaiians represented sixty percent of a total roster of twenty-five servants.

The fishing at Fort Langley, which was done mainly by local Indians using their traditional weirs, was so good that in 1828 McMillan reported: "We could trade at the door of our fort I suppose a million of dried salmon if we chose enough to feed all the people of Rupert's Land,"[5] the vast HBC-controlled territory from Hudson Bay to the Rocky Mountains. In time, fishing became more important than farming at Fort Langley. In 1830 a cooper was brought to the fort to make barrels from pine staves cut on the opposite shore of the Fraser. A profitable trade developed in salted salmon, which was shipped mainly to Hawaii. This amounted to 200 to 300 barrels per year during the 1830s, 800 in 1845, and 1530 barrels in 1846. Salmon salting and packing peaked at 2610 barrels in 1849, which required an enormous output from the fort's cooperage. Peeohpeeoh was the first of the Langley Kanakas to practise the trade of cooper, for which he earned an extra three pounds (above his basic pay of seventeen pounds). In 1850, at the peak of salmon exporting, another Kanaka, Ohia, became a cooper. Later, Peeohpeeoh's son Joseph Mayo, who began his HBC employment as an apprentice labourer in 1847, also worked as a cooper at Fort Langley.

The expansion of the Kanaka work force mirrored the growth of Fort Langley itself. By 1838 the first post had become overcrowded, so work began on a new fort two miles upriver, in part to be closer to the best farmland. But in April 1840 this fort was destroyed by fire. A third fort was built in 1841. It had a large stockade surrounding a cleared grassy area and specialized workshops as well as living quarters for officers and servants. This is the establishment that has been partially rebuilt and opened to the public as a heritage park.

A dominant concern during Fort Langley's first two decades was relations with the Indians. Governor Simpson wrote that

> the great population of this part of the country and the hostile character they bear, renders it necessary to send a larger force among them

than the trade in the first instance justifies. We are only respected by these treacherous savages in proportion to our strength and means of defense.[6]

In the first year of the fort's existence, a Fort Langley party led by chief trader Alexander McKenzie was attacked and killed by Clallam Indians while camped on the shores of Puget Sound. A punitive expedition of sixty men, including at least two Kanakas manning canoes, was sent to find the culprits. It was supported by the firepower of the HBC ship *Cadboro,* with its six Kanakas. A history of the Langley area recounts the grim results: "Two families of Clallams were encountered and wiped out. Two men, two women and four children [were] killed. It was never ascertained if they knew anything about the killing of McKenzie."[7] Later the *Cadboro* located the main party of Clallams and blasted their village with its cannons, after which company men landed and torched the remaining huts. A count revealed that seventeen Clallams had been killed.

Tribes from an extensive area came to trade at Fort Langley, yet throughout the early years relations with the Indians remained tense. One incident that illustrates the edginess of the fort's commander concerned a Kanaka who was subject to seizures. At the end of August 1830 the man, identified as Maniso, suffered a seizure while washing up in the Fraser after a day's work in the fishery. He wandered about, lost and helpless, and observed by local Indians. He tried to get food from them, and to seize a canoe. They drove him off, and he disappeared into the woods. An Indian reported this to chief trader Archibald McDonald. But when days passed and the Kanaka did not appear, the officer was convinced the Indians had murdered him. McDonald made plans to attack the Indian village, but the Kanaka stumbled into the fort just in time to prevent this atrocity.

McDonald encouraged his men to marry Indian women, which he thought made them more likely to renew their contracts for another year. By 1830 both Como and Peeohpeeoh had done so and had signed up for two more years. According to one account, McDonald did not let them bring their Indian wives into the fort, so the Kanakas built their own homes across the river and paddled to work each day. They settled in the area of present-day Maple Ridge between Haney and Albion near a stream that came to be known as Kanaka Creek. Recent excavations at the third Fort Langley indicate, however, that Kanakas had their own house within the fort's stockade, separate from the dwellings of Euro-American employees. Most likely this represented the situation in the later years, when security was no longer such a concern. The separate housing may have been used not by permanent servants and their families, but by transients associated with the fur brigades that travelled to and from the interior.

Marriage was also an adjunct to gift-giving and gunboat diplomacy in relations with the Indians. According to Jason Allard,

> it was the custom in those days to encourage marriages between the employees of the company and native women. Some were married according to the Indian custom, but afterwards, on the arrival of the priests, were remarried. . . . Mr. Yale was very particular about getting the men married into good families amongst the Indians for the protection of the fort.[8]

In one such case, in 1847, Yale registered the intention of a Kanaka named Keavie to take an Indian woman named Katey Squissum as his "lawful wife" and "to have the marriage ceremony duly and evangelically solemnized on the earliest opportunity, when a clerical person may be had to perform the same."[9] The witness was the Kanaka Ohia who later became a cooper.

As at all HBC installations, daily life for Fort Langley's servants was tough. As Jason Allard recalled,

> All work started at 6 a.m. and ended at 6 p.m. rain or shine, and as a matter of fact, all were kept at work the year round with a half holiday on Saturdays, which really meant scrubbing quarters. . . . One can hardly realize the amount of work which was performed by these men from year to year and at such small wages, £30 to £50 per year—without a strike ever being heard of![10]

In fact, the wage in the early years for ordinary labourers was only seventeen pounds, rising to twenty pounds in the early 1850s (after the California Gold Rush created a scarcity of labour on the Northwest Coast) and to thirty pounds in the late 1850s and early 1860s.

The main relief from drudgery was drinking. Again, Jason Allard provides the most vivid account:

On ration day (Saturday) at noon the workmen were given a gill of pure rum (gratis). They also were allowed to purchase a pint apiece for the Saturday night spree. There were bootleggers even in those days among the men. Those who did not drink did a flourishing business on Sundays for the sick ones purchased what rum had been saved by the non-drinkers. . . . All work ceased on Christmas Eve. The men were treated to a gill of rum and were then allowed to make purchases for themselves and wives. On Christmas morning all the employees of the fort, dressed in their very best, marched in a body up to Mr. Yale's [the chief trader's] quarters—it was called the big hall. Mr. Yale usually received them kindly and held a sort of smoker for a couple of hours in which the decanter was passed around freely. When at last they were feeling pretty happy they were told to go to the ration shop, where they were issued ducks, geese, beef, venison, peas and tallow. Sandwich Islands molasses and a small allowance of tea were added to the bill of fare. Day and night, the dancing was kept up and there were no fancy dances in those days, the more noise the merrier.[11]

Allard then describes an incident that reveals much about the frontier pecking order of whites, Kanakas, and Indians:

In the afternoon of Christmas Day the men's wives [all of them were, of course, Indians] were invited to the big hall where they were given two or three "shots" of wine after which their baskets (they were told to bring them) were filled with cookies, cranberries and blueberry jam and ships bisquits. As soon as the women got outside, the fun started as the wine had put the fighting spirit into them. The women who were married to white men were related to the chiefs and the line was drawn between them and the wives of the Kanakas. The Kanaka women were accused of passing remarks about their white sisters and then from one imaginary insult or slight the fight was on. There was no prancing and sparring. It was run and grab for the hair of the head. A regular tug-of-war ensued. Finally they were separated by their husbands and all was peace and quietness.[12]

Fort Langley may have been a rough frontier outpost, but life there was apparently good enough to satisfy its Kanaka employees. They married, or lived common-law with, local Indian women and kept reenlisting. In many cases, they and their children remained in the Fort Langley area for the rest of their lives (see Chapter 11). Of the ten Kanakas who worked at Fort Langley in 1842–43, for example, only two returned to Hawaii when their contracts expired.

❋ ❋ ❋

If farming, as opposed to fur trading, was important to Fort Langley's role, the same was true to an even greater degree at two other posts where many Kanakas served. The sea link between Forts Vancouver and Langley required ships to cross the treacherous Columbia River bar, navigate a fog-shrouded and rocky coast devoid of safe harbours and enter the current-torn inner waters of the Strait of Juan de Fuca and the Strait of Georgia. But there was an alternative canoe route, which had been taken by the initial exploratory party to Fort Langley in 1824: up the Cowlitz River from the Columbia, across a short portage, then downstream to Puget Sound. The HBC developed this important communications link with the help of Kanaka labour.

Trading posts with good agricultural potential were established at Cowlitz (roughly halfway between the Columbia River and Puget Sound) and at Nisqually, near today's Tacoma, Washington. In 1839 the HBC created a subsidiary, the Puget Sound Agricultural Company, to manage these farms. As on the farmland at Fort Vancouver and Fort Langley, Kanakas did much of the manual labour. At Cowlitz Farm, where some 1000 acres were put under cultivation, Kanakas worked the fields, built a stable and house, and split rails for the sheep pens. As one historian notes, "They were even willing to work on holidays, which was considered to be '. . . much to their credit.' "[13] The high point of Kanaka employment at Cowlitz was probably 1844–45, when sixteen Hawaiians worked there, out of a total of twenty-six servants. This declined by 1847–48 to nine Kanakas, along with ten other labourers, mainly French Canadian. In 1849–50 there were five Kanakas (along with six French Canadians), as the HBC gradually withdrew from what was by then United States territory.

At Fort Nisqually, established in 1833, the situation was similar. In 1842–43 ten Kanakas served at the post, which developed large flocks of sheep and thousand-strong herds of long-horned cattle to feed the HBC's Pacific operations and supply Russian settlements in Alaska. As late as 1850–51 there were six Kanakas working the farm, three of whom

John Kahana with Lummi wife Mary Skqualup and stepson Robert Bull, San Juan Island, Washington. (Center for Pacific Northwest Studies, Western Wash. Univ.)

had been there for a decade. A Kanaka named Cowie, who had an Indian wife, worked at Nisqually as a shepherd at least from 1842 through 1855 and was still on HBC books in 1859. But part of the work force (perhaps those without families) was shifted around among the forts and farms as needed. For example, a Kanaka named Ehu worked as a labourer for three years (1844 to 1847) at Cowlitz Farm, then three more (1847 to 1850) at Fort Vancouver, returning to Oahu in 1850. Another, with the similar name Ehoo, was a midman at Cowlitz Farm for three years (1840 to 1843), then a midman at Nisqually for a year and a labourer at Nisqually for four years (1844 to 1848) before returning to the Islands in 1848.

Indians were hired to work alongside the Kanakas at Nisqually, but at the much lower pay of four to eight pounds per year. Long-serving Kanakas like Cowie earned seventeen pounds per year during the 1840s. By comparison, British shepherds at Nisqually made thirty-five pounds. Here is an obvious example of the middling position the Kanakas held in the fur trade pecking order—somewhere between the locally hired Indians (who owed no loyalty to the HBC and were easily replaced) and the whites. As the HBC was forced out of American territory, the Nisqually farm shrank in importance, but it remained in operation until 1887.

Some of the Kanakas who had worked there retreated north into British territory with the HBC. Others married local native women and settled in the Puget Sound area. For example, according to his great-granddaughter, a Kanaka named John Kalama collected furs for the HBC and

Charlie Kahana, son of John Kahana and Mary Skqualup, circa 1930.
(Center for Pacific Northwest Studies, Western Wash. Univ.)

later worked for the company at Cowlitz Prairie constructing fish barrels for the shipment of salmon. John married one of the five daughters of the Chief of the Nisqually tribe, Mary Martin, who lived in a big long house on Muck Creek [Yelm, on the Nisqually River, upstream from today's Nisqually, Washington]. For her hand in marriage, many blankets, beads [and] clothing [were] demanded. . . . He died about 1870.[14]

A study of Kanakas in Washington State shows that many descendants of Hawaiians remained there long after the withdrawal of the HBC and its agricultural subsidiary.

One notable individual was the blind fiddler Charlie Kahana of the Bellingham area. Kahana was descended from a Kanaka who married into the Lummi Indian band, whose territory is just south of the Canadian border. An excellent photo from 1930 shows him as a distinguished old man, dressed in a straw boater hat and playing his fiddle.

6

The Siberia of the Fur Trade

F or all the hazards and humiliations of HBC service, Kanakas enjoyed relatively stable living and working conditions at the posts that had sizeable farms—Forts Vancouver, Langley, and Nisqually, Cowlitz Farm and, later, Fort Victoria. In many cases they stayed at a single post for long periods, married local native women, and established lasting ties with the neighbouring Indian bands. They and their descendants often settled near those posts when they ended their HBC service.

The situation was quite different farther north. In the 1830s and 1840s the company established a network of more remote fortified trading posts on the north coast of what was to become British Columbia. Most of these had little or no agricultural potential and were little more than extremely isolated stockades with Indian encampments outside the walls. The HBC also had posts in the northern interior. Kanakas served at all of these more remote posts, but on average for much shorter periods. Weather and living conditions were harsher than at the agricultural settlements. There was far more frequent turnover of men, less frequent marriage with native women, and much more trouble.

The first (and longest-operating) north coastal post was Fort Simpson, where Kanakas served from 1831 to 1860. Established first at the mouth of the Nass River, but after two years relocated nearer the Skeena, Fort Simpson was initially staffed with twenty-three Kanakas, one of the largest contingents at any HBC post other than Fort Vancouver. Nearly all of these men were newcomers to the company, a sign that well-established Kanaka employees resisted being sent off to endure the long, rainy winters and gloomy days near the tip of the Alaska Panhandle. Indian lodges sprang

S.S. Beaver *ten miles from Fort Simpson.*
(Courtesy Vancouver Maritime Museum)

up around the new fort. Theft by natives and other threats to security meant that the gates had to be kept locked from sunset to sunrise. The HBC men felt themselves to be under siege. Because of its extreme isolation—nearly five hundred miles north of the nearest post, Fort Langley—Fort Simpson was for the first few years assigned an armed ship with a largely Kanaka crew to help protect it and to defend the HBC trading monopoly on the north coast against trespassing American vessels.

By 1837, not one of the original group of Kanakas was still at Fort Simpson. Through the 1840s very few Kanakas worked there but in the early 1850s, after a near-mutiny at Fort Rupert (see below), a group of Kanaka malcontents was sent north to the fort, probably to isolate them from their colleagues. But they, too, got away as soon as they could. Unlike other HBC coastal posts that operated for decades, Fort Simpson does not seem to have had a single Kanaka who stayed, married locally, and left descendants in the area.

In 1833 the HBC established Fort McLoughlin, on Milbanke Sound just north of Vancouver Island's northern tip, and gave it a work force that included nine Kanakas, nearly all of them transferred from Fort Simpson. It was another forbidding place of dark, brooding forests. William Tolmie, the trader and physician there, wrote in his journal that wolves were numerous in the hills behind the fort. But efforts were made to keep spirits up.

Tolmie recounted how the men celebrated New Year's day of 1835. To get the festivities rolling, each "received a couple of drams [of rum]." That evening the men assembled and "danced with great vivacity till 10 to vocal music." The Canadians "sung several paddling songs. Our two Iroquois danced the war dance with great spirit of their tribe and the S[andwich] Islanders sung Rule Britannia tolerably well." A couple of days later, there was a boxing match between an Iroquois and an Islander. "The latter floored his opponent neatly and came off the victor."[1] Fort McLoughlin was closed in 1843, when Fort Victoria was built, and the Kanakas were transferred to the new post.

※ ※ ※

A post with an unusual history was Fort Stikine. Founded as an outpost of the Russian-American Company on Duke of York Island along the Alaska Panhandle, it was leased by the HBC in 1839 and physically taken over by the company in 1840 under an agreement designed to exclude the Americans from the far Northwest Coast and assure the Russians of supplies from the Columbia Department for their remaining posts in Alaska. Under the Russians there had been thirty-two men stationed at Stikine, plus a gunboat for defense. The HBC left only a single officer in charge and eighteen men. By 1842–43 this contingent was increased to twenty-two, eleven of them Kanakas and the rest Canadians and Iroquois. Governor Simpson reported that Fort Stikine was "maintained by fish and venison which are procured in great abundance from the natives at a very cheap rate."[2]

Stikine did not prove to be a peaceful place. In 1842 John McLoughlin Jr., the commanding officer, was shot dead by a voyageur named Heroux during a drunken orgy. Governor Simpson, who arrived only a few days later, dismissed the crime as "justifiable homicide"—McLoughlin Jr. had allegedly ordered two of the Kanakas to kill Heroux—and turned the man over to Russian authorities at nearby Sitka. According to a subsequent investigation, however, two Kanakas, Captain Cole and Kalepe (or Kakepe), had witnessed the killing. All the men at the fort, except a Kanaka named Pouhow, had allegedly signed an agreement to murder McLoughlin because he would not allow his men to have Indian women in their rooms overnight and punished those who stole HBC goods and gave them to the women.

Simpson refused to press the case, presumably because of his personal rivalry with the dead man's father, John McLoughlin Sr. The accused conspirators were never brought to trial. Many of the same Kanakas from Fort Stikine would make trouble for the HBC years later, when they were posted to Fort Rupert. As at Fort Simpson, the turnover of men at Fort Stikine was very rapid.

※ ※ ※

In 1840 the HBC also established Fort Durham (or Taku), located even farther north than Stikine on Taku Inlet, which cuts through the Alaska Panhandle. Finding himself surrounded by high mountains, one of its first officers, Roderick Finlayson, called Fort Durham "as dismal a place as could possibly be imagined."[3]

The first year it rained or snowed nine months out of twelve. And the natives were none too friendly. An American trading vessel had engaged in battle with the Indians a few years earlier and killed many of them. The Indians thought the HBC men were Americans and on one occasion attempted to "take the fort and murder us all." A Kanaka "gatekeeper" tried but failed to keep out one of the warriors. Finlayson was bludgeoned but, armed with pistols, he managed to gain control of the situation, and gunfire from the fort's bastions eventually frightened the Indians away.

Finlayson was happy to be transferred the following year, but eight Kanakas stayed on at Fort Durham until, in a cost-cutting measure, the fort was closed down in 1843. It must have been a great relief to the Kanakas when most of them (along with the men from Fort McLoughlin) steamed south on the *Beaver* to sunnier climes at the new Fort Victoria.

※ ※ ※

Fort Rupert, near present-day Port Hardy on northern Vancouver Island, had a different raison d'être than the other posts. It was built in 1849 primarily to protect some newly discovered coal deposits, and secondarily to fill the gap in the HBC trading network left by the abandonment of Fort McLoughlin. Coal had become important because of the growing number of fully or partially steam-driven ships on the Northwest Coast. The initial work force consisted of thirty-five Canadians, Kanakas, and Englishmen. As one officer wrote, there was "a great deal more of French and Kanaka spoken than other languages." Another noted, ominously, that never before had "such a miserable set of devils" been congregated.[4]

The HBC brought proud miners out from Scotland, some with families, to work the shallow coal seams. But their voyage around the Horn and

Hudson's Bay Company's establishment at Fort Rupert, 1866.
(HBCA/PAM P-111/N5296)

up to the Northwest Coast was a miserable ordeal. And they were forced to do what they saw as demeaning work while delayed en route at Fort Victoria. Arriving at last at Fort Rupert, they found their living and working conditions to be far harsher than they had expected. The last straw for some was being ordered to dig a drainage ditch under a Kanaka's house. They called it "a place with the smell hardly fit for a pig to go in"[5] and refused to work. The officer in charge imposed a harsh fine, so the Scots went on strike.

Inept leadership by HBC officers, a steady supply of liquor from a visiting ship, and rumours of the wealth that could be earned in the gold fields of California turned the strike into a veritable mutiny. Conditions bordered on anarchy. Canadians and Kanakas boozed it up. Wild shooting went unpunished. When the gold fever really hit, the strike spread to the English and French Canadian labourers.

Kanakas were valued by the HBC for their loyalty, but even they succumbed to the mutinous atmosphere. Eight of them—mainly a group that had been transferred from troubled Fort Stikine and whose contracts had expired—demanded to be allowed to leave Fort Rupert and head for California. They were refused permission. Under the terms of their agreement, they were obligated to remain at work until an HBC vessel could return them to Hawaii.

Some of the Scottish miners and English labourers slipped away from the fort. Twelve employees deserted in June and July of 1850. But none of them was a Kanaka. Whether through coercion or persuasion, the group of disgruntled Islanders with gold in their eyes was shipped north to Fort Simpson and signed to new three-year contracts.

Seven other Hawaiians (including several who play interesting roles later in the Kanaka story—see Chapter 8 for Joe Friday, Chapter 12 for Jim Kimo, and Chapter 16 for Bill Mahoy) stayed on at Fort Rupert into 1851 or 1852. By then, life at the fort had become a bit more civilized. Land had been cleared and planted, so there was some fresh produce, while the Indians supplied fresh meat in exchange for trade goods such as blankets, cotton, tobacco, and beads. Recreation consisted of target shooting as well as horseback riding, at which the Kanakas excelled. Some Canadian and Kanaka servants had married women from northern Indian tribes, and the fort had spawned a surrounding shantytown of Indian huts.

Given a few more years of growth, Fort Rupert might have given rise to a lasting Kanaka-Indian community. But the fort lost much of its importance when more easily worked coal seams were found farther south along Vancouver Island under today's city of Nanaimo. Some of the Kanakas were transferred to Nanaimo, leaving only a few at Fort Rupert, which stayed in operation as a trading post for Kwakiutl territory. The last Kanaka, Kamano (also known as Kaumana), remained at the fort until 1869–70. (For Kamano's story, see Chapter 13.)

❀　❀　❀

The northern posts from Vancouver Island to Alaska were aimed at the trade with coastal Indians. In the vast interior between the coastal range and the Rocky Mountains, however, there was also great fur potential. The posts there—the HBC districts of New Caledonia and Thompson's River— were initially linked across the Rockies to the HBC empire of Rupert's Land. But with the growth of Fort Vancouver, the interior districts came to be connected to the Pacific by the brigade system. Each year's outfit of trade goods and other supplies was sent up the Columbia by boat, transferred to pack horses for portage to the Fraser, and then transferred again to canoes (and in some cases horses or dog sleds) for distribution to the far-flung interior posts. Annual returns of furs came down out of the interior in the opposite direction by the same tedious route, which took up to four months each way. This link to the Pacific meant that Kanaka labour, although concentrated on the coast, was sometimes assigned to interior forts according to company needs.

As early as 1822–23, Como (the long-serving but not-very-eloquent cook; see Chapter 5) and another Kanaka named Canot worked at Fort St. James, the headquarters for New Caledonia (on Stuart Lake, just west of the Rockies in north-central B.C.). Both men were still there in 1825. Como was then transferred to Fort Langley, but Canot stayed in New Caledonia and died there in 1834. Throughout the 1840s the Fort St. James journals refer to "Oyhees" cutting firewood, building boats, and the like. Their numbers gradually increased. In 1847–48, for example, nine Kanakas worked in New Caledonia and an additional three in Thompson's River. By then, as Fort Vancouver was phased out, the interior brigades no longer reached the Pacific by way of the Columbia, but via an equally difficult route along the Coquihalla River to the lower Fraser and down to Fort Langley.

The climate in New Caledonia, which was quite unlike the temperate coast, must have been especially hard on the Hawaiians. Winters were intensely cold and the lack of local agriculture meant a monotonous diet consisting largely of dried salmon. The chief factor arranged musical soirées to entertain the men but this did not prevent the district's earning a reputation as "the Siberia of the fur trade." One historian characterizes life in New Caledonia as "one of gruelling and relentless labour, oppressive punishment of resistance to authority, and precarious subsistence."[6] The nutrition was so inadequate that an HBC officer wrote: "Seldom any man, even the most robust, without destroying his constitution, can remain in New Caledonia more than two or three years."[7]

Life on the brigades involved not only long days of paddling, but also lugging ninety-pound packs of trade goods and furs across long portages. Not surprisingly, some of the men tried to desert. In 1847 two Kanakas left an inland-bound brigade to New Caledonia, and their treatment was merciless:

> The next thing was to punish the deserters. . . . Our guide, a tall, powerful Iroquois, took one of them and Mr. Lewis seized the other. . . . [T]he punishment consisted in simply knocking the men down, kicking them until they got up, and knocking them down again until they could not get up any more, when they finished them off with a few more kicks.[8]

Kanaka employment in New Caledonia tapered off, from nine in 1847–48, to seven in 1848–49 and three in 1850–51. With the decline of Fort Vancouver and the routing of brigades through Fort Langley, Kanakas who had served at New Caledonia and Thompson's River were posted to forts and farms in what is now coastal B.C. One Kanaka, Namhallow, remained in New Caledonia until 1861. Another, Tahowna, was transferred back and forth between New Caledonia and Thompson's River from 1847 to 1851, the last year earning a gratuity for working as a cook. As with the Kanakas on the north coast, those who served in the interior left few descendants, place names, or other evidence that men from distant islands had ever paddled the rock-strewn rivers or trodden the snowy mountain trails.

7

As Black as Your Negroes of the South

B y the mid-1840s several dozen Kanakas were serving at HBC posts in what is today British Columbia. Many of them were long-term employees who married local women, raised families, and remained in B.C. for the rest of their lives. Far more Hawaiians, however, were working at Fort Vancouver and other posts south of the forty-ninth parallel. Kanaka employment at Fort Vancouver peaked around 1845 to 1846. Yet even as it did, the company's days in the southern part of the Oregon Country—and the days of its Kanaka servants—were numbered.

A growing stream of American settlers, travelling in covered wagons, braved the Oregon Trail in the early 1840s to reach the promised land of the lush Willamette Valley. By 1845, the population of western Oregon was around 6000, only about 1000 of whom were British subjects. The American doctrine of Manifest Destiny proclaimed the expansion of the country from coast to coast to be a political imperative. Texas was annexed in 1845, which soon led to war with Mexico. During that war of convenience, American forces captured and occupied much of California, which became de facto part of the United States, though it formally entered the union only in 1850.

In the election campaign of late 1844 the rallying cry of the victorious candidate, James K. Polk, was "fifty-four forty or fight." This would have meant the annexation of the entire Oregon Country, from northern California at forty degrees latitude to Alaska at fifty four. After Polk's election, however, a compromise was worked out in the Oregon Treaty of 1846, which left Britain the territory north of the forty-ninth parallel plus Vancouver Island (which protrudes slightly south of that line). The islands between Vancouver Island and what is now northern Washington (today's Gulf and San Juan Islands) were to be divided along a line following the middle of the main channel to the Pacific Ocean. This sowed the seeds of a later dispute that affected the lives of many Kanakas (see Chapter 8).

Although the Treaty of 1846 granted the HBC "possessory rights" to the land it already occupied, it placed the company and its servants in an untenable situation and ultimately forced them out of what had become the Oregon Territory (today's states of Oregon and Washington). As one study of Fort Vancouver notes,

> What started out as a thin trickle of American settlers into the area [around Fort Vancouver] turned into a surging flood of homesteaders who either settled on acreage which had been cleared and cultivated by the Company, or built on land claimed by native Indians. The inevitable conflicts between settlers and Indians gave rise to fears of a bloody, full-scale Indian uprising, so when the United States Army requested the Company's permission to establish a post adjacent to Fort Vancouver the Company agreed.[1]

The army and HBC soon fell into disagreement over the meaning of "occupied land" and "possessory rights," and bit by bit the HBC found its property encroached upon. Fort Vancouver was gradually phased out, dwindling from around two hundred employees in 1846 to only fourteen by 1860.

The last of Fort Vancouver's Kanakas to go was the teacher/minister Kanaka William, whose house was burned down by United States soldiers in 1860. This caused a minor diplomatic crisis in which Britain sent letters of protest to President Buchanan in Washington. The "Kanaka William incident" hastened the abandonment of Fort Vancouver. By then, Fort Victoria was already the HBC headquarters on the west coast, and remaining personnel were transferred there. William himself remained on the company payroll as a relatively privileged "assistant" in Victoria until 1868–69, working in the sales shop (probably as a clerk, as he could read and write) and earning up to sixty pounds in wages plus forty pounds more in "gratuities and sundry credits." During this period he lived in the James Bay section of Victoria. His wife died in Victoria in 1865, but whether William himself died in Victoria or moved away and settled elsewhere is unknown.

The other Kanaka employees of the HBC in the Oregon Territory were also forced to make choices by the pressure of American settlement and the gradual withdrawal of the HBC north of the forty-ninth parallel. Many left HBC service when their contracts expired, and a few deserted even sooner. This trend was greatly accelerated when gold was discovered in California in January 1848. In 1848 and 1849 at least thirteen Kanakas deserted.

Kanakas already in North America were well situated to get involved in the gold rush, and they did, leaving their names at several places called Kanaka Bar, at Kanaka Glade in Mendocino County, Kanaka Creek in Sierra County, and Kanaka Dam on the Yuba River. Hawaiians also left the Islands to join the feverish quest for instant riches. These included even such elder notables as Thomas Hopoo, who had been educated in Connecticut and helped establish the first Protestant mission in Hawaii (see Chapter 1), and William Kanui, who had travelled around the world in 1809, fought in the U.S. Navy against the Tripolitanian pirates of North Africa, taught school in California, and operated a restaurant at Fort Sutter. Kanui made a small fortune of six thousand dollars in the gold fields, then lost it, and eventually returned to Hawaii to work as a teacher.

So many Islanders headed for California—over two hundred by October 1849—that the kingdom's government passed a series of laws designed to restrict the outflow. But many of those who found their way to the creeks and river bars had already been on the west coast and had deserted from other employment. As Janice Duncan noted in her study of Kanakas in the United States:

> Suddenly, Kanaka labor began disappearing as the Islanders joined the exodus to the gold fields. John Sutter lost his Kanakas, as did the HBC. . . . They did have some success in the gold fields, but had no social standing and frequently were involved in conflicts with the other miners because they preferred to dive for the gold in the rivers rather than use conventional methods.[2]

Not all of these Kanakas were victims, however, and some used unconventional—and unlawful—methods of their own. One of Fort Sutter's Kanakas, Jim Crow, specialized in swooping down on Chinese gold miners and robbing their sluice boxes. He eventually reformed, married an Indian woman, and became a law-abiding salmon fisherman. In 1871 he became an American citizen and in 1880 a voter in Sutter County.

Many of the Kanakas who joined the California Gold Rush probably found cause to regret their decision. Life at HBC forts was regimented and gruelling, but on the gold frontier they were hardly welcomed with open arms. A history of the Kanakas in California notes: "The Hawaiians suffered indignities at the hands of the Anglos in the same fashion as the Californios, Chilenos and Chinese . . ." The state legislature imposed licensing fees on foreigners, and some of the enforcement officers were corrupt.

> When the officer appointed to grant these licenses and collect the fees came to Kanaka Dam, he in reality came "to jump their claims," an American miner reported. Coming with a large posse to back him up, he refused to accept the license money offered him by the Kanakas with the excuse that it was now too late to receive it, after he had summoned a posse. Ironically, many members of the posse accompanying the collector, W. B. F. Royer, were themselves foreigners. Claims taken from the Kanakas were given to [them]. Captain Coxe, the head chief of the Hawaiians at Kanaka Dam, told Royer that the three-month license which he had paid for on Bear River was still good and in full force, but he was ignored. Finally Royer tried to make a deal with Captain Coxe, but the latter refused, since Royer "had driven off his men, and they had gone nobody knew where."[3]

If this is the John Coxe who came to the Columbia River on the *Tonquin* in 1811 and served the HBC at Fort Vancouver, it is his last appearance in the historical record.

❋ ❋ ❋

In 1850 the first census in the newly established State of California counted 319 Hawaiians. Along with blacks, Chinese, and people of other races, they were in direct competition for jobs with the dominant white majority, and the backlash was not long in coming. In 1852 the California senate passed a resolution to exclude "Chinese or Kanaka carpenter, masons, or blacksmiths, [brought to California] in swarms under contract to compete with our own mechanics, whose labor is as honorable, and as well entitled to social and political rights . . ."[4]

In Oregon Territory, discrimination against Kanakas had appeared even earlier. In 1845 the provisional government's legislature considered instituting a tax of five dollars per head on the introduction "into Oregon Territory of any Sandwich Islanders . . . for a term of Service"[5] and an annual three-dollar tax on Kanakas already employed and not returning to the Islands. The first Oregon census of 1849 did not count Kanakas at all, just as it ignored Indians and half-breeds. That same year, when some Kanakas applied for American citizenship in order to vote in the election, they were turned down on racial grounds.

Most important of all, on a frontier where free land was being distributed to settlers, Kanakas were excluded. In 1850, the first Oregon delegate to the United States Congress, Samuel R. Thurston, introduced an amendment to a resolution relating to Oregon land grants. It provided that a grant of land be made to "every white male settler or occupant of the public lands, American half breeds included," but not to "members and servants of the Hudson's Bay and Puget's Sound Agricultural Company." Thurston argued against giving land to anyone connected with the HBC,

> including some hundreds of Canakers or Sandwich Islanders, who are a race of men as black as your negroes of the South, and a race, too, that we do not desire to settle in Oregon. Whatever falls into the hands of these men would be just so large a windfall to the Hudson's Bay Company.[6]

Denied citizenship and land, many Kanakas either returned home to the Islands or followed the HBC north to British Columbia as it gradually liquidated its activities and holdings south of the forty-ninth parallel.

There were exceptions, however. One Kanaka mining colony, on Indian Creek in El Dorado County, California, survived until 1862. It consisted of twenty-four people, most of them pure Hawaiians, including two Hawaiian women, three Indian women, and four half-Indian children. A visitor noted, "Two of the squaws spoke Hawaiian correctly, all dressed neatly and were busy cutting, sewing, washing and ironing the family clothes. One of them was busy reading the Hawaiian Bible."[7]

At La Grange there was an even larger colony, with about forty Kanakas, as late as 1868. It was visited by a Congregational minister from Hawaii, Reverend J. F. Pogue, who found them in a "cold, dead state," drinking like whites and without religion or thought for their souls. "Gold is their god, as it is the god of many a white man,"[8] he concluded. Pogue asked if they wanted to go back to Hawaii, but they said they had no money for the trip and did not really want to return.

In 1870 a new gold rush began on the Klamath River in Oregon, and many Kanakas went there to work some of the hundred or so placer mines. One of the Kanaka-owned mines remained in operation until 1885 and gave rise to a proper little colony, with a Kanaka school and cemetery. As happened in British Columbia, many of the Kanakas who stayed in Oregon and Washington married native women and blended into the local Indian communities.

8

Twenty Kanakas Brandishing Knives

With the withdrawal of the Hudson's Bay Company from Fort Vancouver and other operations south of latitude forty-nine, Fort Victoria on southern Vancouver Island became the HBC's western headquarters and its main depot on the Pacific coast. The fort and its satellite farms employed dozens of Hawaiians. Later, the city of Victoria became a social and administrative centre even for Kanakas who did not actually live or work there. Between 1849 and 1870, for example, Victoria churches recorded at least eight baptisms of part-Kanaka children, fourteen marriages involving Kanakas or part-Kanakas, and fifteen burials.

Even before the fort was established, however, there was Hawaiian blood on southern Vancouver Island in the person of Songhees Indian chief Cheealthluc, who had a Hawaiian father or grandfather.

"King Freezy," as he was called by the whites owing to his frizzled hair, an inheritance from his Kanaka or Hawaiian progenitor, was very friendly to the whites. But he was "in disgrace" with the Royal Navy, having walked off with the [ship] Thetis's cashbox on the pretext of taking it to show his wife.[1]

A lively history of Vancouver Island describes him, even less kindly, as a "half-breed yes-man" who was under the thumb of the HBC. "No wonder he was detested by the Haida, who shed no tears when 'King Freezy' drowned, drunk, on November 11, 1864."[2]

From the very start, Kanakas were a major part of the work force at Fort Victoria. Chief Factor James Douglas arrived from Fort Vancouver in

1843 to select the site for the new establishment (initially called Fort Camosun), then proceeded north on the *Beaver* to Forts McLoughlin and Durham to close those outposts. Governor Simpson had decided that those remote areas were not profitable enough and that trade there could better be carried out through occasional visits by the highly mobile steamship. Three of the Kanakas from Fort Durham were transferred to Fort Stikine. Douglas brought the rest of the men—including eight Kanakas—with him when he returned south and assigned them to help build the new fort and to serve there. Fort Victoria was considered highly vulnerable to Indian attack and was initially given a large complement of thirty-four servants and two officers. (By 1850–51 this had expanded to sixty-two men, sixteen of them Kanakas.)

Once the large stockade—over three hundred feet on each side, with a tall bastion and cannons commanding Victoria Harbour—was completed, many of the Kanakas were put to work on nearby farmland in an attempt to

Construction of Fort Victoria, 1843.
(HBCA/PAM/Newton Brett/P-407/N11685)

S.S. Beaver *off Fort Victoria, 1846.*
(HBCA/PAM/Adam Sherriff Scott/P-397/N7151)

feed the new outpost, as well as to supply HBC (and later Royal Navy) ships. One of the farms, at Constance Cove between Victoria and Esquimalt harbours, came to be known as the Kanaka Farm. By 1854 there were thirty-four people living at this farm, which was run by the Puget Sound Agricultural Company, or PSAC.

Kanakas were also sent to work on San Juan Island. Today the island belongs to the United States, but at the time it was claimed by Britain and was so close to Victoria that it was a popular destination for Sunday picnic excursions. The fate of the San Juan Island Kanakas became inextricably linked to the outcome of the conflict that arose over the island's ownership. According to the Oregon Treaty of 1846, the United States-British border between Vancouver Island and the mainland of what is now Washington State was to follow the main channel to the sea. Britain maintained that this meant Rosario Strait, to the east of San Juan Island, which would have made the island part of today's Canadian Gulf Islands. The United States claimed that Haro Strait, between San Juan Island and Victoria, was the key channel. The dispute took practical form in 1853, when the British informed an American settler (who had been cutting timber on San Juan Island) that he was trespassing.

Chief Factor James Douglas, by then also the governor of the colony of Vancouver Island, became alarmed that an influx of Americans would lead to a challenge to British sovereignty. According to one history of Victoria, Douglas sought British settlers to populate San Juan, but none had the inclination "to go off pioneering in these remote, Indian-infested islands whose very nationality was open to question.[3] Determined to impose a British presence, Douglas decided to establish the Belle Vue sheep farm on San Juan Island under the auspices of the PSAC. In December 1853 the *Beaver* dropped off the farm's first foreman, Charles J. Griffin, and a band of Hawaiian shepherds to care for a flock of thirteen hundred sheep.

The United States countered by planting the American flag and stationing an American officer on the island. The following year a Washington Territory sheriff named Barnes was sent to San Juan with a group of assistants to seize some of the HBC's sheep (which the Americans claimed had been brought to the island illegally, without customs being paid) and to auction off others to cover taxes which the United States claimed was owing on the PSAC's property. When Barnes and his men were leaving "there was a whoop from the hill and Griffin, together with some twenty Kanakas brandishing knives, were seen charging down toward them."[4] But Barnes's men drew their revolvers, so Griffin and the Kanakas beat a hasty retreat.

The conflict became more serious when an American settler killed one of Griffin's pigs, which had been rooting up the American's potatoes. This led to a thirteen-year comic-opera stand-off known as the Pig War. Nobody was killed, but both Britain and the United States garrisoned troops on the island. During this time the Kanakas lived and worked mainly on the southern end of San Juan Island, where there is still a Kanaka Bay. In 1865 the Hawaiians at the sheep farm still numbered around twenty.

Eventually the matter was submitted to the German kaiser for arbitration. In 1872 he decided the issue in favour of the United States, and the PSAC was forced to abandon its sheep farm. Most of the Kanakas, aware of the opportunity to pre-empt land and obtain citizenship and voting rights in British Columbia, chose to leave San Juan Island and settle just across the border in the Gulf Islands, especially on Salt Spring (see Chapter 14).

Among the Kanakas who are remembered on San Juan Island was Joe Poalie, better known as Joe Friday, who had first worked for the HBC at

Cowlitz Farm around 1841 and remained on the company books through 1859–60. He had a shack near the water's edge on the eastern side of San Juan and grazed his sheep near what is today the island's main settlement, Friday Harbor. (Smoke from his chimney guided early boatmen, who came to call the large, sheltered bay "Friday's Harbor.") Other Kanakas who lived on San Juan Island during the period of the dispute—and who later moved to the Gulf Islands—were Kama Kamai, William Naukana (also known as Lackaman), and William Nawana. During the Pig War period, some San Juan Island Kanakas were listed in Victoria city directories and went to Victoria for such events as baptisms and weddings.

$$\text{\Large ✴ \quad ✴ \quad ✴}$$

Aside from doing farm work, Kanakas served at Fort Victoria as stevedores, watchmen, sawyers, and domestic help. They also served in the small and short-lived militia of the new Colony of Vancouver Island. As the Victoria *Daily British Colonist* commented sardonically in 1861:

> In the good old days of Victoria, if five or ten years ago can be called old days, a corps of "Invincibles" was formed here, composed of eleven Kanakas and two negroes. . . . It was found that our diminutive Colonial exchequer was much too small to support such an immense standing army, and they were consequently disbanded.[5]

The Victoria Voltigeurs, as the militia was called, was set up in 1851 and existed for seven years as a mobile rifle corps to defend settlers throughout the colony and especially to guard Fort Victoria from the danger of Indian attack. Governor Douglas used them frequently, together with HBC seamen, on forays to apprehend Indians who had killed whites or otherwise seriously threatened law and order. In the first successful instance reported by Douglas,

> we learned that the murderer . . . was concealed in the woods, on the sea coast, about 3 miles distant. The pinnace [ship's boat] was immediately despatched with 16 seamen, and 9 half whites [the Voltigeurs], towards that point where his place of refuge was soon discovered and after a long chase in the woods in which the half whites, took a principal part, the wretched man, was captured and taken on board the Steamer "Beaver."[6]

The Cowichan Indian and an accomplice were soon tried, sentenced, and hanged, the first such execution in British Columbia.

During the mid-1850s the Voltigeurs were often used on more routine patrol duties on horseback "to visit the isolated settlements for their protection."[7] In 1856, eighteen Voltigeurs were sent as part of a large expedition to Cowichan after the attempted murder of a white man by a Cowichan Indian. Again the alleged culprit was captured and executed. After the Fraser Gold Rush began, the white population increased dramatically and the Voltigeurs were disbanded. As late as 1857 and 1858, however, the force included at least six Kanakas: Ebony, Juano, Tom Keave, Balan, Tamaree, and Pakee.

When the gold rush hit, the HBC's status changed dramatically, and with it the situation of its Kanaka employees. Just as the influx of settlers spelled the end for the HBC in Oregon, when gold was discovered on the Fraser River in 1858 the HBC's monopoly was doomed. The flood of miners and the economic boom that followed overwhelmed the company, leading to the founding of the Province of British Columbia and the opening up of land for pre-emption and sale. This sweeping change offered the resident Kanakas new opportunities and led eventually to their dispersal to private land pre-emptions, sawmill work, and other employment.

The impact of the gold rush was felt first in Victoria, which only a few years earlier had been a sleepy fort surrounded by a few farms and Indian villages. Modern steamships meant, however, that Victoria was no longer isolated. When news of the gold finds spread, steamers from San Francisco brought thousands of eager miners to Victoria in a few weeks. The town's population (which had included only 232 non-natives at the end of 1854, plus another 154 on the four PSAC farms) doubled and doubled again. As Harry Gregson writes,

> with the arrival of the gold seekers the settlement swarmed with open latrines, tents, lean-to's, negroes, Kanakas, Chinese, Jews, Frenchmen, Englishmen, Germans and other nationalities. . . . [They] congregated like birds of a feather . . . the Jews on Johnson Street, the Chinese in nearby "Little Canton," the Kanakas on Kanaka Row (now Humboldt Street) and the negroes wherever they could find room.[8]

Kanaka Row was little more than a line of shacks facing a stinking mud flat at the very head of Victoria Harbour. This tidal flat was later filled in and is now the site of the venerable Empress Hotel, which opened in 1908.

As the town grew, the forest had to be felled to clear the way for roads. "All the heavy labour was done by Indians and Kanakas . . . the latter being expert axemen."[9] By 1862 Victoria had become a town of jerry-built wooden houses and stores with a permanent population of some twenty-five hundred.

> The demand for lumber and carpenters for the construction of hotels and saloons was insatiable and many abandoned farming or the Hudson's Bay Company service to satisfy the demand or to seek his fortune in the gold-diggings.[10]

Some of those who headed for the gold fields were apparently Kanakas. Nothing is known about who they were or how many, but they left their name at Kanaka Bar on the Fraser just below Lytton.

The Kanakas were ranked toward the bottom of the growing town's social ladder, a big step above the Indians (who were not considered part of mainstream society at all) and the Chinese (who were not to gain the right to vote in British Columbia until 1947) but below many other nationalities. Because of this, there is little trace of them in the newspapers of the day. They were mainly noticed when they ran afoul of the law. In 1860, for instance, the Victoria *British Colonist* reported that

> Palew, a Kanaka, became enraged at one of his countrymen the other night, and to revenge himself, went to the latter's residence, and smashed in all the windows of his house, for which he was arrested, and made to pay 2 s[hillings] and costs of court, 4 s; besides give security for his future good behavior.[11]

Years later, by which time the currency had changed, the newspaper ran a brief notice about "Lassaro, a Kanaka, charged with supplying liquor to Indians, on remand from the 16th inst, was fined $20."[12]

On another occasion, the *Daily British Colonist* reported on a "rather ludicrous scene."

> A Kanaka who had been very ill for some time was believed to be approaching his end, and his comrades, moved by excessive fore-thought, gave an order to the undertaker to provide a coffin. The un-

dertaker assuming that the poor fellow was dead, called in at the cabin and proceeded to measure what he supposed to be the corpse, when to his horror, the sick man sat up in his bed and glared wildly around him. The coffin was made, however, and not much too soon after all, as the man died on the second day after he had been measured.[13]

9

On His Hawaiian Majesty's Service

The Fraser Gold Rush and explosive population growth led quickly to the end of the HBC's trading monopoly and to the founding of the Colony of British Columbia in November 1858. Some HBC posts remained in operation on a reduced scale for decades longer, but the company closed its office in Honolulu, and recruitment of Kanaka labourers ceased. By then, nearly all of the Kanakas who had worked at posts in British Columbia had left HBC service for other work. Most of them had lived in North America for many years, had married native women, and had fathered children. Few of those who served into the 1850s took the HBC up on its contractual commitment to return them to Hawaii. Legally, however, they remained initially subjects of the king of Hawaii, and their interests were at least formally protected by Hawaiian consulates. But what was their personal and emotional relationship to their homeland or, in more modern terms, their ethnic identity? And why did so few return home to stay?

The establishment of frequent commercial passenger service between Victoria and Honolulu (directly and via San Francisco) meant that even after leaving the HBC Kanakas could have gone back to the Islands, either to stay or simply for a visit. Shipping records indicate that private individuals with Hawaiian surnames did make the journey. And according to descendants of William Naukana, an HBC servant who later settled in the Gulf Islands, he went back to Hawaii after his stint with the HBC and then returned to the Northwest Coast (see Chapter 14). HBC records show that at least twenty-six Kanaka servants made trips home under company auspices during their years of service and then returned to company work. A few made two such trips home.

There was also regular mail service to and from Hawaii—one or two ships a year even during the early years of HBC isolation on the Northwest Coast, and many more once settlement began. Even if many Kanakas could not read or write, they could have had letters written for them, perhaps by literate co-nationals, such as the teacher/minister Kanaka William. Like immigrants from other lands, they could well have remained in contact with their families and may have retained other links to the old country.

One letter that has survived gives a good sense of the continuing Kanaka attachment to Hawaiian culture and customs. It was written by (or for) William Naukana to describe a traditional luau held on Puget Sound at Port Gamble, Washington, in 1865. The occasion was the birthday of Pilipo, son of John Kao'o (probably the former HBC servant John Kaau, who had worked at Victoria in the mid-1850s, at the same time as Naukana) and Kao'o's wife, Mary Pau. Naukana describes the "large rectangular lanai," or covered veranda, that was built for the occasion, and the "eating mat" covered with white linen cloth. When the food—taro *poi* imported from Honolulu, pig, fish, and *haole* or white foods, such as tea, coffee, and bread—was ready, "the drum was sounded . . . calling the multitude to come and eat." Another Kanaka, Joe Kaaawa (Ka'a'awa), blessed the food "in the name of the holy one who dwells in the heavens," and the first group—the Hawaiians—began to eat.

When the Hawaiians had finished, the eating mat was set again, the drum sounded and the *haoles* were invited to eat

> whatever they wanted. When they were through they expressed their gratitude at what the Hawaiians had done here . . . and for being able to witness the feast. And it continued all day, a new thing at Port Gamble. This marked the first of the good things done by the Hawaiian children (here at Port Gamble). Let it be continued so all from Hawai'i to Ni'ihau [outermost of the major Islands] will know.[1]

As Victoria grew in population after 1858, it also became an important port for the increasing commerce with Hawaii. A Victoria directory noted in 1862 that

> steam communication is carried on three times a month between San Francisco and Victoria. . . . A steady and increasing trade is carried on

with S. Francisco, the Sandwich Islands, Oregon, Washington Territory and the coast of British Columbia.[2]

In the first half of that year, imports to Victoria from the Sandwich Islands amounted to $96,643, which compared quite favourably with the $115,608 imported from Washington Territory and $168,825 from England.

The kingdom of Hawaii established formal consular representation in Victoria, as well as at nearby Port Townsend, Washington, just across Juan de Fuca Strait. The first Hawaiian consul at Victoria was a merchant named Henry Rhodes, who was of British birth but had lived for some time in Hawaii and knew the language. Rhodes arrived in Victoria in June 1859 and became friends with Governor Douglas, who appointed him to the Legislative Council of Vancouver Island. When Rhodes died in 1878, he was replaced as Hawaiian consul by Robert Paterson Rithet, a prominent Victoria merchant.

Rhodes (and later Rithet) was there not only to promote trade between British Columbia and Hawaii, but to help Hawaiian subjects who found themselves in trouble. Rhodes became involved, for example, when a Kanaka was sentenced and executed for murder in 1869 (see Chapter 10). Earlier, in November 1866, two Hawaiian seamen and a Hawaiian female passenger were shipwrecked with the Hawaiian-registered barque *Mauna Kea*—outbound for Honolulu with a shipment of lumber from Puget Sound—on the west coast of Vancouver Island. They were fed by local Indians until they could be rescued. Rhodes reported the incident to the Hawaiian Foreign Office and requested permission to send the Hawaiians home at government expense and to pay the costs incurred.

In 1879, Victoria Consul Rithet wrote a letter to the Foreign Office in Honolulu (headed "On His Hawaiian Majesty's Service") requesting instructions regarding two "native Hawaiians" who wanted passage home by steamer. "In one case," he wrote, "the applicant had sufficient money to pay it but appeared to think it was my duty to provide the passage for him. In the other case, the applicant had no funds."[3] The same letter discussed the case of John Henry Keahalaka, a native Hawaiian subject, who had applied at Victoria to re-register a Peruvian ship as a Hawaiian vessel.

Across Juan de Fuca Strait, a few years later, the Hawaiian consul at Port Townsend, Washington Territory, was called upon to pay the medical and living expenses of an aged and indigent Kanaka named Nuheana (or "Kanaka Jack") and to arrange his passage home to Hawaii. Nuheana had landed in Victoria in 1858 or 1859 and had found work in Port Townsend. In 1872 both his hands were crushed in an accident at the bakery where he was working, leaving him a "county charge" for thirteen years. Finally, in 1886, Jefferson County, Washington billed the Hawaiian consulate for over five thousand days of room, board, and medical expenses. The county auditor described Nuheana as "a man of good moral character, and a most deserving person."[4] Nuheana himself claimed that his father had been a servant of Hawaiian King Kamehameha I. The Port Townsend consul arranged the man's passage home (for thirty dollars), paid a sizeable hospital bill, and asked his government for instructions as to what portion of the huge $4,816.50 bill for food and lodgings it felt obligated to pay.

The consul in Victoria played a ceremonial role when Hawaiian Prince Lot arrived with his entourage from Honolulu in September 1860 on board the *Emma Rooke,* which the *Daily British Colonist* described as "one of the most beautiful little schooners eye ever beheld." Henry Rhodes was there to greet the ship and go on board. The prince was then quartered at the French Hotel, and though he was in poor health he met some of Victoria's "prominent citizens."[5] Press reports did not mention whether he deigned to meet any of his ordinary Kanaka subjects. After a week-long stay, Prince Lot departed for California, but the Victoria press continued to report in extravagant terms on the travels of this "distinguished" royal personage.

❋ ❋ ❋

Would news of such a royal visit have instilled pride or tugged at the heartstrings of Kanakas living in the Victoria area? Perhaps, but it is unlikely that many would have wanted to give up their new lives in British Columbia. None of the pomp and glory could have disguised the fact that, by 1860, Hawaii was no longer the same society that these now-middle-aged Hawaiians had known as children. And it had long since ceased to be a South Seas paradise, if indeed it had ever been that, except in the eyes of sex-starved sailors and European and American artists and writers.

Pre-fur-trade Hawaii was a highly stratified and hierarchical society dominated by a small class of chieftains. One early European observer concluded that the commoners were not happy people: "The artisans and farmers . . . are . . . condemned to work almost continually for their lords . . . without hope of compensation and restriction even in their choice of foods."[6] A strictly enforced *kapu* (taboo) required women to eat separately from men. Below commoners was a smaller class of inferior status who were

The changing face of Hawaii: Honolulu, 1857.
(HBCA/PAM/G.H. Burgess/1987/363-H-27/3/N11684)

dominated by their masters and were, in the words of an American anthropologist, "ritually polluting to aristocrats."

> Above the commoners was a noble class that filled all important political offices, and worked only minimally for their own support. . . . Membership in all classes was inherited, and genealogies were the major determinant of social rank.[7]

Island chiefs controlled all resources and,

> by right, could dispossess any commoner of the properties he used. Many commoners owned no land and drifted about. Tribute was due to a chief from all people living within his jurisdiction; and they were also required to labor at public works undertaken by the paramount chief.[8]

The growth of the fur trade, bringing with it exposure to Western technology and values, led to the rapid breakdown of that society. First came the deliberate breaking of the taboos by the ruling nobles in 1819. Then, Western missionaries were successful in implanting Christianity—and its sectarian divisions—with great speed. Christian marriage, for example, was only introduced in the early 1820s but was compulsory on some islands by the end of that decade. Economic change also proceeded very rapidly. According to a student of Hawaiian history,

As a growing number of trading vessels anchored at the islands a noncompetitive economy of subsistence was transformed with brutal rapidity into a forced economy of trade. The sandalwood trade with China, which flourished in the first two decades of the nineteenth century, brought increasingly oppressive labor conditions.[9]

A Hawaiian demographer summarizes the situation to 1850:

Catastrophic depopulation occurred on all the islands. . . . Declining birth rates and high infant mortality rates altered the age distribution of the people. Young men went to sea and never returned. Foreigners began to take up residence . . . and at the end of this period Hawaii was on the threshold of its first influx of indentured laborers.[10]

Village life also gave way to rapid urbanization. In the 1840s and 1850s, foreign whites began to dominate the political, economic, and religious life of the Islands, largely in alliance with native chiefs and the royal family. After 1840 whites could own land. By the 1850s white foreigners ran government ministries, banks, and shipping lines. Soon large-scale introduction of foreign (mainly Asian) indentured workers changed the ethnic face of Hawaii forever. Between 1850 and 1930, some 400,000 people were brought to the Islands "as a result of the sugar planters' relentless search for cheap and docile laborers."[11]

Little wonder, then, that Kanakas who had gone abroad and put down roots might be reluctant to return to a homeland that was becoming unrecognizable. William Naukana, who fondly described the luau of 1865, is an example of one who apparently did go home, compared the societies, and opted for life on the Northwest Coast (see Chapter 14). Kanakas in British Columbia may not have enjoyed high social status. But as their service with the HBC ended, they were free to live and work where they pleased and to acquire land on favourable terms.

Eventually, they could become naturalized Canadians and exercise the right to vote, serve on juries, and hold public office (which some did—see Chapter 11 for the story of George Apnaut). They may have retained some of their Hawaiian customs, but it is doubtful that many longed to go back to a country that was no longer truly their own.

10

Seduced by the Instigation of the Devil

he Kanakas of British Columbia had a low-profile but generally positive image in the public mind, such as it was in the early days of the new crown colony and province. They were viewed (somewhat patronizingly) as reliable, honest, and hard-working employees, albeit somewhat happy-go-lucky and occasionally inclined to excessive drinking. This rather benign reputation took a beating when two particularly nasty multiple murders, only a few years apart, were committed by Kanakas.

The first took place at Nanaimo, the fast-growing coal port and second-largest community on Vancouver Island (after Victoria). Kanakas worked there for the HBC in the 1850s, in most cases after first serving at Fort Rupert. One was a flamboyant night watchman named Jim Kimo or Keamo (see Chapter 12). Another was Kahua, who worked at a sawmill on the Millstream River and was known as an excellent salvage diver. Whenever a coal barge sank, his job was to dive and attach chains and ropes to the hull, so it could be lifted on the next high tide. He left Nanaimo in 1859. There was also Tamalee (also known as Thomas Tamaree or Komaree), who had worked at Fort Rupert, served as a Victoria Voltigeur, married an Indian woman while living in Nanaimo, and later settled in the Gulf Islands.

And then there was Peter Kakua, or Kanaka Pete, who had come from Honolulu to join the HBC service in 1853, working first at Fort Vancouver, then at Victoria and Fort Rupert. After five years at Fort Rupert he moved back to Victoria, where he claimed he had worked for Sir James Douglas for a year and at a variety of jobs for several more years before joining the crew of the steamship *Labouchere*. Finally he took a job with the Vancouver

Coal Company in Nanaimo. There he lived with his common-law Indian wife of about six years, Que-en (also known as Mary) of the Penelakut band from the southern Gulf Islands, and their daughter.

According to Pete's later testimony, in late November 1868 his wife left him for several days and sent a message that she no longer intended to live with him. He began to drink heavily and went home intoxicated on the night of December third around midnight, expecting to find the house empty. Instead, he found his wife and her parents there. His wife said she was there only to collect her things. Pete went out to get some more whisky from a friend and returned to his house, where he found his wife in bed, having sex with her father. Infuriated, he tried to pull the father off his wife, but the older man grabbed his hair and bit off the tip of his finger. His wife's mother rushed at him and began beating him on the head and body with a stick, and his wife joined in the fracas as well. "Being considerably intoxicated at the time," his translated testimony continued, "and owing to the pain I was suffering I became almost mad and laid hold of the first thing I could reach which was an axe [produced in court] and laid about me indiscriminately."[1] Then he lost consciousness.

The screams and sound of blows were heard by a neighbour, who did not investigate, however, because it was 2 A.M. and domestic fights were common in the neighbourhood. When Pete awoke he found that he had slain his wife, both her parents, and his baby daughter.

Pete went to his friend Tamalee, told him what had happened, showed him the stump of his finger as proof and said he was going away. Not believing him, Tamalee went to the house and found the bodies. With some delay, he reported his findings to the authorities. By this time, Pete had set off by canoe for the mainland with an "African" who had apparently been drinking with him. The black man changed his mind about crossing the Strait of Georgia and asked to be let off at Newcastle Island, which shelters much of Nanaimo Harbour. They built a fire, drank some more, and were captured easily when a search party of special constables appeared on the scene.

A coroner's inquest was convened in Nanaimo and, based on Pete's own confession, Tamalee's confirming testimony, and the grisly evidence of the corpses, concluded that Pete had murdered his family. It also recommended a merciful sentence, but this was later torn from the original copy of the proceedings, and the note was added that such a recommendation was "not in the province of a coroner's inquest."[2] Pete was sent to jail in

Victoria to await his trial. The magistrate in charge of the case sent a letter to the colonial secretary noting that the victims' tribe was distressed by the crime and wanted to see the murderer executed.

Several Victoria lawyers took part in Pete's defense. The prosecution made a number of technical errors that allowed them to challenge the Crown's case. When the trial convened in February 1869, Pete pleaded not guilty to "wilful murder," and was tried on two counts by two separate juries, composed entirely of white men. (The city's juror's list included six Hawaiians.) Pete's main defense was that he had felt no ill will toward his wife and acted in a fit of passion while under the influence of alcohol.

On the count of murdering his wife the jury found him guilty, but recommended mercy on the bizarre grounds that "Kanakas are not Christians and killing men may not be such an offense in their eyes." The jurors believed that Pete, "not having the fear of God before his eyes" had been "moved and seduced by the instigation of the devil."[3] On a second count, of murdering his wife's mother, Pete was found guilty without a recommendation for mercy, largely because her body was found in a position indicating that she had been trying to hide. Some observers at the time concluded, however, that it was the killing of the baby that really sealed Pete's fate. He was sentenced to hang, and appeals for mercy by Henry Rhodes, the Hawaiian consul in Victoria, were in vain.

Pete was returned to Nanaimo to be hanged at dawn on March 10, 1869 at Gallows Point on Protection Island. A Victoria newspaper wrote: "He ascended the scaffold unflinchingly, made no remarks, and struggled but slightly after the drop fell."[4] Pete was buried on Newcastle Island near where he had been captured, a lovely spot behind the beach at what is now called Kanaka Bay. But he did not rest in peace. In 1899, coal company employees inadvertently unearthed the coffin while digging a mine shaft on Newcastle, and the remains were examined and identified. Finally, Pete's body was reinterred in an unmarked grave on Newcastle, which is now a popular marine park, picnic ground, and campsite. To this day, park wardens tell the sad story of Kanaka Pete to easily spooked children as they sit around the campfire, and warn that his ghost still haunts the island.

A few years after Pete's trial and execution, Victoria was shocked by another grisly crime committed by a Kanaka, this time on nearby San Juan Island. After the 1872 settlement that awarded the island to the United States, many of the Kanakas moved across the new border to Salt Spring and its adjacent islands. But some remained on the southern end of San Juan in a cluster of shacks at Kanaka Bay. These included two teenaged brothers, Joe and Kie Nuanna. Joe, born at Oregon City in the Willamette Valley, had grown up and attended school on San Juan Island and had not been considered particularly troublesome.

In June 1873, a farmer named William Fuller was found murdered. He had been shot and bludgeoned. A few days later, a neighbour found James Dwyer, a farmer, dead in his field, the back of his head smashed in. His pregnant wife, Selina Jane Dwyer, was found dead inside the house, where the door and a window had been broken. Although San Juan Island was now American territory, the bodies were taken to Victoria for funeral and burial. The islanders went into a state of shock and fear of their neighbours, especially when an investigator sent from Victoria announced that the culprit was probably a white man. Bootprints had been found, and the local Indians (who had committed several murders in the Gulf and San Juan islands in the 1860s and 1870s) rarely wore shoes.

One woman, however, recalled that before the Fuller murder Joe and Kie Nuanna had asked to borrow a shotgun, along with a pouch of shot, to go pigeon hunting. Joe had returned the gun, but acted strangely, and the woman had found bloodstains on the gunstock. When questioned by local Justice Warbass, she remembered that he had not returned the pouch. Inquiring at Kanaka Bay, Warbass learned that the Nuannas had gone to Victoria "to have a time," so he telegraphed the Victoria police. Joe was strolling down Yates Street when he was arrested and questioned about the Dwyer murders. He tried to blame it on an Indian friend, who was then also arrested in Victoria along with another Indian who was suspected of several unsolved killings.

The Indians turned out to have adequate alibis, but Joe's hobnailed boots perfectly matched the tracks found at the Dwyers's farm. In trying to implicate his Indian friend while claiming to be an innocent bystander, Joe had told of two watches stolen from the Dwyers and hidden on Victoria's Kanaka Row, where the police quickly found them. To cap the case, the shot pouch, which Joe had borrowed, was soon found on the Dwyer property. Confronted with the evidence, Joe confessed to the murder of Fuller and both of the Dwyers.

In October Joe was taken in chains aboard a ship and extradited to stand trial in Port Townsend, Washington Territory. The evidence given by his San Juan neighbours was conclusive and after a three-week trial he was sentenced to hang in March 1874. It was the first execution in Port Townsend, and was treated as a gala event. Visitors arrived from all over, and the saloons did a land-office business. A reporter covering the hanging was shocked to find the culprit to be a "mere boy" of nineteen. Accompanied by two sheriffs and a Catholic priest, Joe went almost jauntily to the gallows, doffed his cap and said, "People, I am very sorry for what I have done. Now I have to go. All hands—good-bye."[5] But he was so small and light that his neck did not break, and he slowly strangled before a horrified crowd of hundreds. Port Townsend never had another hanging.

II

"Free Kanakas" on the Fraser

Although some Hawaiians and their children stayed with the HBC (or the PSAC) beyond the late 1850s, most left the company and settled in clusters along the Fraser River, on Burrard Inlet, and, a decade later, in the Gulf Islands.

Even before the gold rush, a few Kanakas settled as squatters west of Fort Langley at the site of the first fort. This area on the south side of the Fraser was called Derby when it was briefly considered as a location for the capital of British Columbia. An observer who stopped at Derby in January 1859 found living there "a large body of Kanakas—a mixed race half Indian half Sandwich Islanders."[1] Their apparent leader was old Peeohpeeoh, by then in his early sixties and Fort Langley's longest-serving Kanaka. He had worked for the North West Company and then the HBC for a total of forty years, at least until 1856–57. At Fort Langley he had married a "sub-chief's" daughter and fathered at least three children. Living there with him in 1859 were his son Joseph Mayo and two sons-in-law, Peter (Ohule) and Ohia. They were evicted when it was decided to sell town lots at Derby for the new capital. Peeohpeeoh then petitioned the government for forty-seven acres on the north shore of the river in compensation. This request was overtaken by events the following year, when a new pre-emption law allowed Peeohpeeoh and other Kanakas to acquire land on their own.

By the late 1850s, far more Kanakas were living independently along the Fraser than remained with the company. But some probably continued to do occasional work for the HBC. In July 1857 Peter Ohule, one of only two Kanakas still working at the fort (the other was Joseph Mayo) was returning to Langley from Victoria. He was asked by James Douglas to mention ". . . to the free Kanakas on the route, that you would require them for the trip to Fort Hope. . . . There are seven able men among the number."[2] It is not clear whether these seven "free Kanakas" included a small group that had settled at Tsawwassen, near today's huge B.C. Ferries terminal. When the United States-Canadian border was being laid out in 1857, an American member of the Northwest Boundary Survey visited the Tsawwassen village and found "a small settlement consisting of a few Kanakas & Indians."[3]

In 1860 land was made available for settlement, and Kanakas were allowed to participate on equal terms with whites. Under the pre-emption act of 1860, all that was required to gain initial possession of a quarter section (160 acres) was to take an oath of allegiance to the sovereign, stake out the corners of the property and pay a two-dollar registration fee to the nearest magistrate. Then the land had to be "improved," which usually meant clearing part of it for farm use—a gruelling task without power equipment—building a house and barn, and erecting fences. Eventually, title to the land could be obtained for one dollar per acre.

In February 1860 four Kanakas appeared before a magistrate in New Westminster and registered nearly contiguous 160-acre pre-emptions on the north side of the Fraser. (The area was across the Fraser from the old fort site and just to the east of an HBC sawmill.) One of the new landholders was Peeohpeeoh. The others were William Tokoa, Tee, and Peter Apponette (also known as Apnaught or Apnaut), whose pre-emption was taken over in 1873 by his son, George Apnaut.

Somewhat later a second-generation Kanaka, Robert Wavicarea, settled in the same area and had at least seven children. His father, known simply as Wavicarea, had served at Fort Langley since 1830, and Robert was born there and baptised by Bishop Demers in 1841 at age six.

Peeohpeeoh's son, Joseph Mayo, joined the group that held land north of the Fraser in 1870. Mayo was another child of Fort Langley who spent virtually his entire life in the area. While in his teens he began to work at the fort as an apprentice labourer in 1847. A powerful young man, he was probably assigned to carry heavy packs of trade goods on a brigade into the northern interior. After two years at New Caledonia (1850 to 1852) he returned to Fort Langley, where he took up his father's trade of cooper and remained in HBC employment until 1860. Physically, he must have been an impressive man. Jason Allard, also a child of Fort Langley, recalled that "Mayo . . . was reputed by the Indians to be the strongest man on earth." As late as 1915 he was still living in the area and was "still active, despite his ninety odd years and a few days ago was out in his boat fishing."[4]

Other Kanakas also settled north of the Fraser. A man named Peter Mayho, who had a Hawaiian-born father, farmed there in the 1880s. He was about ten years younger than Joseph Mayo and was likely his brother. In 1881 a nineteen-year-old fisherman named John Mayhua lived near Peter Mayho in the farm household of Sophie and William Nelson that included George Apnaut. In 1891 a man named James Schell, whose father was born in Hawaii, lived there with his wife and two children.

There was also a large family named Cheer (also spelled Chier) that included three second-generation Kanakas, Daniel, Joseph, and Thomas, and a young man named George Beebe, whose father was also Hawaiian-born. All the men in the Cheer household were fishermen. Some of the Cheers stayed in the area for many decades, living as part of a somewhat nomadic Salish Indian band that moved frequently between the Langley Indian Reserve #1 at Whonnock and Reserve #2 on the nearby Stave River.

One of Daniel Cheer's sons, Harry (or Henry), a true jack of all trades, is celebrated in Charles A. Miller's book, *Valley of the Stave*. He was a close friend of Miller's and once built him a beautiful cedar dugout canoe in exchange for six fifty-pound sacks of flour. Harry built himself a large smokehouse:

> When the dog salmon were running, he prepared 1200 fish that he and his family had caught. He hung them on crab apple poles within, each one held open by small wooden skewers so that the smoke [could] reach every exposed cut part during their curing.[5]

Harry was a passionate deer hunter and sometimes worked as a faller for Miller's family, which owned a small sawmill. He knew many natural medicines, using skunk cabbage root to cure nausea in horses, and the hearts of blue grouse (along with bear gall and balsam pitch) to treat diabetes and asthma in people. Harry also played the clarinet beautifully, but secretively, and only when no one was close by. "However," Miller writes,

> whenever John Barleycorn was about the silver, sweet strains resounded through the valley. When I last saw the clarinet, it bore little

resemblance to its former self, being dented and battered. I wondered how he made such sweet music.[6]

Harry Cheer died in the mid-1960s (he would have been nearly ninety years old) and was buried at Whonnock.

Life was full of hazards early in this century, and many of the Cheers died before reaching adulthood. Of Harry's sons, Augustus (or "Sonny") was killed in a hunting accident in Washington State, Ernest (or "Russet") was drowned at the mouth of the Stave River, and Raymond died in an industrial accident in the Stave Valley. Harry's younger brother, Jack, worked as a faller during the construction of the Ruskin dam and powerhouse. But he was terribly afraid of dynamite. One day, when a big blast was about to be set off, he and some other men had to hurry across the river to shelter. When they reached the shore, his partners found him slumped over. His fear, the coroner later concluded, had caused a heart attack, and he had died on the spot.

Harry Cheer's niece, Clara, married a man named Benito Miranda, who descended from the Chileans who came to British Columbia in the late nineteenth century while working on ships. Many of them settled and worked in the sawmill at Moodyville (North Vancouver) alongside the Kanakas there. (In fact, Benito Miranda's grandfather was named Timothy Moody.) Clara stayed in the Whonnock area until her death in 1980. Other Cheer family members moved to Washington State in the 1920s, and their descendants remain aware of their Kanaka heritage.

Rather than working exclusively as subsistence farmers or fishermen, the Kanakas who settled in the Fort Langley area may have done other jobs as well. In 1860, for example, Robert Wavicarea worked as a cooper, salting salmon in Chilliwack. According to one history of Maple Ridge, a number of Kanakas from Fort Langley went to work for Samuel Robertson, a white former HBC boatbuilder, who also pre-empted land on the north shore of the Fraser and bought additional property there, assembling an estate of over six hundred acres.

By 1877 three second-generation Kanakas were listed on the municipal assessment roll of Maple Ridge, their 160-acre lots assessed as worth $320 each. George Apnaut had improved one acre, Joseph Mayo three, and Robert Wavicarea five. At first there was no school on the northern shore, and the children had to row across to the school at Fort Langley. But in 1875 a one-room school was opened on the river bank in what is now Maple Ridge. It had sixteen children the first year, one of whom was a Mayo.

In January 1879 George Apnaut was elected to the first Maple Ridge town council. A pioneer later recalled Apnaut playing the violin at local dances, while his sister Mina played piano or violin. But he is also remembered as a brute who abused his young wife, Julia Hamburger. The orphaned daughter of a German-Jewish businessman and half-Indian, half-white mother (the daughter of Fort Langley HBC officer Ovid Allard), Julia was forced to marry George Apnaut by her stepmother, an Indian woman named Sophia Nelson who had previously been wed to George's Hawaiian father, Peter Apnaut. Julia Apnaut soon fled the unhappy relationship for Victoria, where she had the marriage annulled and became a dressmaker. When George Apnaut died, she celebrated by buying herself a red dress.

The Kanakas in the Maple Ridge area probably never numbered more than ten families. When the Canadian Pacific Railway was built, its tracks ran right along the Fraser, and the little riverside community was obliterated. The last house was gone by 1912.

12

A Cabin, a Garden,
and some Cherry Trees

As new work opportunities appeared, many Kanakas moved away from places such as Fort Langley and Fort Victoria that had been familiar to them. But as people who were physically and culturally different from the majority of the population, they tended to settle near other Kanakas and Kanaka descendants. One such area was on the heavily wooded shores of Burrard Inlet where, in the 1860s and 1870s, axes rang as the great forests were cleared at the future sites of Vancouver and North Vancouver.

One of these settlers was a man named Eihu, who is said to have been a teacher in Hawaii. He was married by the factor at Fort Langley to an Indian woman named Mary See-em-ia. Eihu went to work at Hastings Mill (at the edge of present-day Gastown in downtown Vancouver), where he and his wife lived with their pigs and chickens. Eihu also made charcoal (in large pits) for the blacksmith shop at the mill, and his children attended school there. But the mill owner objected to having the animals running around, so in 1869 the Kanaka family moved west along the shore and settled at a pretty place where a small creek ran into Coal Harbour at a large pebble beach. There (where the Westin Bayshore hotel now stands at the foot of Denman Street) they built a cabin and planted a garden and cherry trees. The homestead, which grew to include several houses and outbuildings, came to be known by some as the Kanaka Ranch or Rancherie, and by others as the Cherry Orchard.

Mary See-em-ia Eihu seems to have had children by a second husband as well. In the words of Major J. S. Matthews, the diligent Vancouver archivist who interviewed many Kanaka descendants (among other Vancouver old-timers) during the 1930s to 1950s:

*Kanaka
Ranch, 1904.*
(Teresa O'Leary)

True or untrue, but the story is that at the Kanaka Ranch, there lived an Indian woman who had two husbands. She lived, figuratively, one month with one, next month with the other.[1]

The second husband was generally known as Joe Nahanee, although he was also called Joe Nahano and may have originally had the name Nahinu or Kahinu. According to one descendant, Joe Nahanee had worked for the HBC in Victoria, later owned land there near the present site of the Parliament Buildings, briefly joined the Kanakas who settled on Salt Spring Island, and eventually went to work at Hastings Mill, where he made charcoal and fired the boilers. He died around 1874 and was buried on nearby Deadman's Island and later reinterred in North Vancouver.

Another Hawaiian who worked at the Hastings sawmill and settled at the Kanaka Ranch was James Keamo (also known as Jim Kimo). A relative latecomer to HBC service, he worked for the company at Fort Rupert from 1850–53 and then at Fort Langley. In the late 1850s, he lived in Nanaimo, where he had a cabin and cabbage garden, and worked for the HBC as a night watchman. According to Nanaimo's first mayor,

Jim [Kimo] dressed gaily, wore a bright red sash, tassel in his cap, and seemed quite contented and happy. It was a part of his duty, at 12 o'clock midnight, to fire off a gun and call out "All's Well." He had a drum which he thought much of. He managed to fix an appliance by means of which, on pressing his foot on a treadle, the drum would be struck almost the same instant as his gun was discharged. He amused himself daily by beating the drum as others would by playing some choice-favorite solo instrument.

After sunset, his particular job was to guard the company's large log-built store.

At any hour of the night, and in all conditions of weather, the faithful watchman could be found on duty. . . . Kimo's occupation was abolished in 1860, when he went [back] to Fort Langley.[2]

There—or possibly in the Maple Ridge area—he met and married Annie Nelson, who was of mixed Scottish-Indian blood and was the half-sister of George Apnaut. When they moved to the Hastings Mill, some of the men, finding Keamo too difficult to pronounce or spell, began to call him Campbell. Some of his descendants continued to go by that name, others by Keamo.

With the addition of the Keamos, the Kanaka Ranch population swelled. But by 1889 Keamo, his wife Annie, and their five children had moved to New Westminster, where they had five more children. He earned his living as a salmon fisherman and for a time as a stonemason. James Keamo died in 1905.

Two of his sons, Walter and Harry, went overseas to fight with the Canadian Armed Forces in the First World War. Walter fought at Vimy Ridge and came home in 1919 deaf in one ear. Harry fought with a different unit and came home unscathed.

The Kanaka Ranch was wedged between the sea and rugged bush. Nearby Stanley Park was then still an area where both whites and Indians squatted, some raising cows and pigs, others catching dogfish and rendering them into oil to sell to the mills as lubricants. The Kanaka children made the long walk to the Hastings Mill School, the first on Burrard Inlet, through a wooded area full of lurking sailors, prospectors, and other ne'er-do-wells.

One of the youngsters was Minnie (McCord) Smith, who is celebrated in a history of early Vancouver as "little Scottsie Two-tails" because she always wore neat pigtails and a tartan Glengarry cap. She recalled walking along a trail through the woods: "Oh, I was so frightened! I was only a little girl, and the runaway sailors had shacks in the bushes; they were hiding there, along by where Cardero Street is now.[3] She used to hurry by, crouching and trying not to be seen, or made a detour via the beach when the tide was low.

The Kanaka Ranch itself eventually succumbed to the pressure of urban growth. Eihu, the original Kanaka settler, died there around 1886 and the Keamos moved away, but Mary Eihu stayed on with her children. Then in 1895 a real estate dealer tried to dispossess the remaining Kanakas. The case went to the Supreme Court, which in 1899 sustained the Kanakas' squatters' rights. Despite this judgement, within a few months Mary Eihu wrote to the mayor and city council of Vancouver protesting that the real estate man had

> broken down our fences, destroyed portions of our orchard . . . taken possession of five sixths of our land and . . . destroyed and burned three of our dwelling houses [leaving] some of the family in destitute circumstances.[4]

The family eventually secured title to a single city lot on the site, where they allowed a store to be established, but ultimately sold the lot for use as a shipyard for $23,500.

How did the part-Hawaiian, part-Indian children who grew up at Kanaka Ranch relate to the surrounding society? Minnie McCord Smith recalled being raised mainly by her grandmother, Mary See-em-ia Eihu. Although Mary was a pure-blooded Indian, she always spoke English, dressed in the proper fashion of the day and had accepted many white values and attitudes. She used to tell Minnie "to try and do like the white man did, to copy him, because he knew a lot." She warned her not to "be like a Siwash." "You know how it is," her grandmother would say, "Half breeds either rise or go down: some of them do well; others just go back to Indian."[5]

But the choice—to "go" Indian or white—largely depended on the individual's sex. Most female offspring from Hawaiian-Indian families in British Columbia married white men and assimilated into white society. Nearly all men from such families married Indian or part-Indian women, and they often established lasting links with native communities. This pattern is not surprising, given a situation in which there were very few white women. By necessity, it was routine for white men to marry Indian or part-Indian women. But it was very unusual for the scarce "respectable" white women (some of whom were specially brought over from Britain on "bride's ships") to marry a dark-skinned man, whether Indian, black, or Kanaka.

Thus, Margaret Eihu (the daughter of Eihu and Mary See-em-ia Eihu) married Benjamin Cameron McCord, a white man who came to British Columbia during the Cariboo Gold Rush and later logged at Jericho Beach. He never gave up his quest for gold, it seems. He went over the Skagway Trail in 1898, died the following year and, according to his daughter, was given the first Masonic funeral in Dawson City. By contrast, William Nahanee, the son of Mary See-em-ia and Joe Nahanee, married an Indian woman and settled in North Vancouver, where their sons later played prominent roles in Squamish Band affairs and longshoremen's union politics.

As a teenager, William Nahanee already worked on the Vancouver waterfront. One day, the (by then old) steamship *Beaver* was in Moodyville for fuelling, and he and another boy were hired to push wheelbarrows of loose coal from its storage place. The *Beaver* sailed with them still aboard, but the boilers sprang a leak near Bowen Island and the ship had to return to Moodyville. Years later, Nahanee recalled the story in a radio talk.

William Nahanee Jr. (born around 1903) worked as a longshoreman,

was active in the Totem Athletic Club, and was the first employee of the Squamish Indian Band. He lived to age eighty-four and was survived by one daughter, eight sons, and numerous grandchildren, some of whom still work at the band-run Mosquito Creek Marina in North Vancouver.

An older brother, Ed Nahanee (born around 1899) was renowned as a skilled pitcher for the North

Bill Nahanee, 1941, speaking at commemoration of wreck of S.S. Beaver.
(CVA Port. P. 569, N.946)

Shore Indians baseball team. From the age of fourteen he worked on the Vancouver docks, and helped load the last sailing ship from that port. Nahanee retired from dock work in 1946 and became the business agent for the Native Brotherhood of B.C. A biography of his friend and co-worker, Chief Dan George (who rose to stardom in Hollywood), describes Ed Nahanee as "one of the most effective men ever to represent the Native Brotherhood in its quest for Indian rights."[6]

Ed Nahanee was also active in longshoremen's union affairs, which in the years following the First World War involved some violent strikes and successful union-busting, as returning veterans became increasingly militant against closed shops. Nahanee recalled that

> one time the union guys had taken a stand in the union hall, armed with clubs and whatever we could find. There were swarms of soldiers storming the doors, and on the roof of one of the warehouses, three machine guns were trained on us by the RCMP, so close I could practically see down their barrels.[7]

The year 1923 brought another series of violent strikes. Company police clubbed strikers, and mounted police rode their horses up the steps of homes sheltering union men and their families. After six months the union was broken.

In 1967 Ed Nahanee received the Canada Confederation Medal from the federal government for his work on behalf of native people. At his death in 1989 at the age of ninety-one, he was remembered for spearheading "many battles to obtain justice on lands that were taken away [by] various governments."[8] He was buried on the Mission Reserve in North Vancouver. Subsequent generations of Nahanees, a very large extended family, have remained active in the economic and political affairs of the Squamish Band of North Vancouver. They have also made visits to Hawaii and researched their Kanaka roots. Maurice Nahanee, a paddler on the Squamish canoe racing team, hopes some day to take his team to Hawaii and compete against Hawaiian outriggers "on the Kanakas' own surf."[9]

❀　❀　❀

The north shore of Burrard Inlet had what was probably the second-largest Kanaka community in British Columbia, after the Gulf Islands. In 1862 the first sawmill, powered by a water wheel, was established there. Two years later Sewell ("Sue") Moody bought the mill, expanded it, and introduced steam power. In 1878 it was incorporated as the Moodyville Sawmill Company, and the surrounding community was known as Moodyville. One of the main streets in Moodyville was a boardwalk lined with wooden shacks and company bunkhouses and known as Kanaka Row (or Road).

Ten or more first- or second-generation Kanaka families lived in or near Moodyville by the 1880s and 1890s. Most numerous were the Nahus. In the early 1880s Leon, John, and Charles Nahu were all employed as sawmill workers there, and a fourth Nahu worked as a logger at Howe Sound. The surname Nahu is something of a mystery. The HBC employment records do not list that name. Perhaps the closest is a man named Nehoua or Nahoua, who had many children while living in Victoria. But according to one account there was a Nahu at Fort Langley in 1858, and a Mrs. Nahu was said to have been among the first children born at the fort.

Leon William Nahu, born around 1863, embodied the Kanaka predilection (when possible) to marry other Kanakas or part-Kanakas. According to his son, Leon Nahu was three-quarters Hawaiian. That is, Leon's father was pure Hawaiian and his mother—born at Fort Vancouver on the Columbia—was half Hawaiian and half Indian. In the early 1880s Leon Nahu entered a common-law relationship with Mary Haly, who was herself the half-Hawaiian daughter of a Hudson's Bay Company servant and an American Indian woman. Mary had been married by a Roman Catholic priest to a white man who then stole her money and ran away.

Later, she wanted to marry Leon Nahu, but the

Herbert ("Jumbo") Nahu.
(Carey Myers)

priest refused. A Moodyville neighbour recalled a meeting where a vote was held to dismiss a school teacher. Someone objected to Mary Nahu's voting because she was not formally married to Nahu: "And they did not let her vote. I thought it very unkind of them to bring that up. . . . [Leon Nahu] 'ran' that race [of Kanakas]."[10] Mary Nahu's younger brother William Haly later worked on ships as a deckhand and also lived in the Moodyville area. Leon and Mary Nahu had at least one daughter and four sons together. Leon Nahu died in Chemainus on Vancouver Island in 1913.

The Nahus and their descendants remained in the North Vancouver area for several generations. Norman, a son of Leon and Mary, worked as a belter in the Burrard Dry Dock. The youngest son, James, lived in Vancouver and also worked on the waterfront as a longshoreman. Herbert, born in 1891, was called "Jumbo" because of his size. His parents' one-time neighbour recalled him as " 'king of the kids' at Moodyville; not a bully, but he always took charge, and the children did what he said; he was a great big boy."[11] Herbert never formally married, but did live common-law with part-Hawaiian Pauline Kamano (see Chapter 13). He went overseas in 1916 and was badly wounded in the leg and by a shot that entered his throat, cut his windpipe, and came out at the back of his ear. Despite the wound, he lived until 1957, when his obituary called him "one of the last survivors of Kanaka Row in Moodyville."[12]

Aside from the Nahus, there were at least six other Kanaka or part-Kanaka households around Moodyville during the 1880s and 1890s, and possibly quite a few more. Thomas Kamma and William Knowalo were both millhands, and each had at least four children. William Carney, who was probably related to the Carneys who settled on Coal Island in the Gulf Islands (see Chapter 14) was also a sawmill worker. Tombana, a general labourer, lived there with his son and daughter. And there were two others: Mary Nahu's brother, deckhand William Haly, and a longshoreman from the Apnaut family of Maple Ridge.

Kanaka Row must have been a rough neighbourhood. There were several large bunkhouses full of single men in their twenties and thirties, most of them millhands, loggers, and sailors. But Moodyville was no backwater by the standards of the day. There was a school, which the Kanaka children attended. And in 1882 Moodyville was the first area on Burrard Inlet to have electricity.

13

A Kanaka with
Frozen Hands

Although most Kanakas in British Columbia chose to live near fellow Islanders, there were others who did not seem to want or need this kind of group support. One of the most interesting was George Kamano (also known as Cahoomana). The Hudson's Bay Company records list him as a Hawaiian, but one of his descendants believed him to be a native of Tahiti who was educated in England. Kamano was one of the last Kanakas to remain in HBC service, working fifteen years at Fort Rupert, the trading post for Kwakiutl Indian territory. When he left the company it was to work for Roman Catholic Oblate order missionaries under Father Leon Fouquet.

Kamano helped them to build and operate St. Michael's Mission on isolated Harbledown Island, near the mouth of Knight Inlet. A visitor in 1870 found the Mission "holding service to about 40 Indians." It included

> a school house and dwelling house with a chapel attached, a barn, workshop, cowhouse and several outhouses besides clearing about an acre and a half of ground in which a variety of vegetables, fruit trees and medicinal herbs are growing.

Because of the "nomadic habits" of the [Kwakiutl] Indians, "the results have not been great as regards the Indians."[1] Even by the standards of the time, it was a hardship post for the missionaries.

> Their poverty was extreme. They lived mostly on the game and fish they caught, slept on the bare floor, and as in the other Oblate mis-

sions of that time had no other light in the evening than that of their fire, except during the half hour of spiritual reading, when one candle was lit.[2]

Having deemed the mission a failure, the Oblate fathers left in 1874. Kamano remained on Harbledown Island with his wife Pauline (or Polly), said to be Iroquois, and their rapidly growing family of at least nine children. There was no school on the island until 1910, so Kamano's oldest daughter, Mary Ann, was sent away to St. Ann's Convent in Nanaimo, where she was known for her beautiful singing voice and dressmaking skills. She was also fluent in several Indian dialects and acted as a court interpreter when Indians were brought to trial. Mary Ann married Norwegian-born Henry Thames, a shipwright who built the barque *Nanaimo* in 1882, thought to be the largest sea-going vessel built on the coast to that time. They had at least six children.

Two younger Kamano daughters married local men. Lillian wed American-born Silas Olney, who logged on Harbledown with a team of oxen but described himself as a rancher. Maria first married Kenneth McCrimmon, and later Jim Jolliffe, who owned a steam tug for towing logs. McCrimmon arrived in 1892 on a twenty-six-foot sailboat and established a private trading post on Harbledown with his partner, William Herbert Galley. Their customers included the island's 250 Kwakiutl Indians, who continued to follow a nomadic lifestyle. They would go up to the head of Knight Inlet in spring for the oolichan run, then fish for salmon in summer and fall for the canneries that were springing up along the coast.

Pre-empting about 140 acres, McCrimmon built a two-storey house made not of logs, but of milled

George Kamano Sr., circa 1910.
(Carey Myers)

lumber—a sign of creeping civilization. Still, Harbledown was an extremely isolated spot to call home. Maria Kamano McCrimmon acted as midwife at the birth of the Galley children. When a school was finally built it had only seven children at first: three Galleys, two McCrimmons, and two Indian girls.

As with Kanaka offspring elsewhere, although George Kamano's daughters married white men, his sons seem to have married native or part-native women at the largely Indian settlement of Alert Bay. George Kamano Jr. married Mary Ann Wadema in 1892 but died at Alert Bay three years later. His obituary mentioned only that he was a "native," not part Kanaka. Kerry (Carey) Kamano, a logger and fisherman, married part-Iroquois Catherine Lewis Kori (or Oteokorie). Years later, one of their daughters, Pauline, lived common-law with part-Hawaiian Herbert ("Jumbo") Nahu in North Vancouver (see Chapter 12).

A third son, Michael Kamano, married three times, in each case to Indian women. He and his third wife, Annie, spent part of their lives at Alert Bay, where he was a fish buyer and later an engineer at the B.C. Packers fish plant, and part at Harbledown Island. They had no children, but adopted an Indian daughter and moved back to Alert Bay so that she could attend school. They returned to Harbledown in 1945, but spent their last years back at Alert Bay. Michael Kamano died there in 1956 at the age of eighty-six, apparently enjoying good health to the end. His obituary noted that "people marvelled at his age, because until recently he had kept an immaculate garden, cut his own wood and packed it up to his house."[3]

George Kamano Sr., the original Kanaka, had also moved to Alert Bay in his later years and died there between 1917 and 1919 at around eighty years of age. In 1947 small Coffin Island, where the Kwakiutl used to place the remains of their dead in the trees, was officially renamed Kamano Island.

❀ ❀ ❀

George Kamano may have chosen to live apart from other Kanakas, but he moved only a relatively short distance from the HBC post where he had served. William Kanahana, on the other hand, somehow wound up living and working in the farthest northern interior of British Columbia, not far from the Yukon border. There is no trace of other Kanakas in that area. In fact, nothing at all would be known about Kanahana if it had not been for a serious accident that was reported in Victoria's *Daily British Colonist*. His name does not appear in the HBC records, so he may have come to British Columbia as a sailor or in connection with the gold rush.

In 1880 Kanahana was hauling freight, alone, on the Dease River in severe winter conditions. The temperature was forty-five to fifty degrees below zero, and a strong north wind was blowing. He apparently collapsed and was extremely lucky to be found the next day, "almost lifeless" and lying on his sleigh. His hands and arms were severely frozen. Considering the weather and Kanahana's poor condition, "it was difficult to find anyone who would volunteer his services to haul the Kanaka up the river." In the end, however, a good Samaritan named Dick Glenn made the four-day journey—this was considered quick under the conditions—to Laketon. There, destitute, Kanahana was put up in a hotel free of charge and "received every kindness and attention from the proprietors."

A meeting was held at Cassiar to raise money to take him for medical treatment to Glenora Landing, a distance of eighty miles, "at the public expense." In the flowery language of the time, it was considered

> imperatively necessary in the cause of humanity that prompt action be taken. . . . Subscriptions were raised on Kanahana's behalf at McDame's, Thibet and Dease Creeks to assist in defraying the expense of keeping him at Glenora.

It was uncertain, the report continued, "whether the Kanaka will lose his hands, or only a portion of his fingers."[4] Unfortunately, the tale has no happy ending—or ending of any kind. Kanahana's fate did not make the paper, and he disappeared into the same anonymity from which he had emerged so briefly.

✖ ✖ ✖

How many other Kanakas came to British Columbia outside HBC auspices—as Kanahana apparently did—and were never listed in censuses or land pre-emption records? We will probably never know. They could even have attained some prominence without being identified as Kanakas. Such was the case of Owen Forrester Browne, a highly successful captain of paddlewheel steamers. He was unusual, in that his Hawaiian blood came from his mother's side of the family.

Browne's paternal grandfather was a Tahitian who worked his way on a sailing ship to San Francisco prior to the California Gold Rush. There he

Right: Northland Echo, *Captain Browne's last ship on Athabasca River, Alberta, 1940.*
(Leila Johnston)

Below: Captain Owen Forrester Browne.
(Leila Johnston)

found work as a stevedore and, because of his dark skin and difficult Tahitian name, was called "Brownie," or David Browne. Around 1840 Browne married a woman of Spanish background and had three sons. One of them, Owen Wamsley Browne, also went to sea when he grew up. In 1865, on the island of Maui, he met and married a Hawaiian woman named Teresa Aponi. They came to British Columbia and took up residence first near Fort Langley and then in New Westminster. According to his descendants, Owen Browne Sr. and his three sons, Henry, Bill, and Owen Jr., all worked the oyster beds at Point Roberts and helped build the Ruskin Dam. A daughter, Sophie, married a man named Fred Clark. The two oldest sons, Henry and Bill, were killed in a boating accident on the Fraser River.

The third son, Owen Forrester Browne, was a stout, shortish man with black curly hair and a swarthy complexion. His father put him through seamanship school, and he obtained work on the paddlewheel steamers that for decades were the main mode of transportation on many B.C. rivers and lakes. In 1905 or 1906 he became a captain on the sternwheeler *Charlotte,* which he skippered for four years. According to a history of British Columbia's paddlewheelers,

> Captain Browne left the *Charlotte* to take command of the new $53,000 *B.X.,* built by the B.C. Express Company. She proved an outstanding

vessel, with Captain Browne in command during her entire river career. In 1919 her Fraser River days ended when she was holed and sank.[5]

Danger was commonplace in the treacherous rapids of the upper Fraser, where Browne took his ship on regular runs between Soda Creek and Fort (now Prince) George. Earlier in his career, the *B.X.* had been put temporarily out of service "when she struck a rock above the [Fort George] canyon. A 60-foot long, 3-foot wide section was gashed from her hull but watertight compartments kept her afloat until Captain Browne beached her."[6] Another time, Browne ran a race against the newer and larger ship *Conveyor*. He was about to pass the competing vessel and would have won, when his opponent, a Captain Shannon with an "Irish temper," intentionally rammed the *B.X.* That race, it is said, "climaxed steamboating on the Upper Fraser."[7]

After the *B.X.* sank in 1919, Captain Browne became skipper of the Hudson's Bay Company boat *Northland Echo* on the Athabaska River in Alberta. He married Margaret Seymour in 1915 and had four sons and five daughters. Following his career on river boats, he retired to New Westminster, where he died in 1948. He is remembered as a proud, reserved man of the utmost integrity. But according to his descendants, in all his years on the Fraser and the Athabaska, he never mentioned his Polynesian background.

Tom and Leila Johnston, daughter of Captain Browne, in 1943.

(Leila Johnston)

14

"Little Hawaii"

I n 1871 the colony of British Columbia entered Confederation. By then there were several small clusters of Kanakas in the new province, as well as scattered individuals. Only in the Gulf Islands, however, did enough Hawaiians congregate to form a true community, a virtual "Little Hawaii." Only there were they numerous, isolated, and self-sufficient enough to retain some of their customs beyond the first generation. Nowhere else did so many Kanaka descendants marry other Kanakas or part Kanakas and retain a sense of ethnic identity for several generations. And only in the Gulf Islands have so many known Kanaka descendants remained until today. Because of this continuity, there is more complete information about these people than about any other Kanaka group.

On Salt Spring Island, by far the largest and most populous of the Gulf Islands, there have been many stories about the origins of these Kanakas. According to one account, they were sailors who had been forced into service and took the opportunity to jump ship while passing the island. Other accounts say that they were "given" their land by the Hudson's Bay Company in recognition of their long and loyal service. A widely accepted version is that they came as a sizeable and coherent group that had lived together on San Juan Island; when it became United States territory in 1872, they moved the short distance to the Gulf Islands. They preferred to remain under British rule, and under a monarchy, to which they were accustomed. This group was said to be under the leadership of William Naukana, believed by his descendants to be the son of John Coxe, the leader of John Jacob Astor's first Kanakas on the Columbia River. Although there are problems and discrepancies with many of these stories, there is adequate docu-

St. Paul's Catholic Church consecration, Fulford Harbour, Salt Spring Island, 1880. The largely Kanaka community of the area helped build the church.
(Salt Spring Island Archives)

mentary evidence to supplement the memories passed down by Kanaka descendants and to sketch a fairly complete picture of life at British Columbia's only true Hawaiian "colony."

By the late 1860s, Salt Spring Island had been sparsely settled for ten years. It was a patchwork of small subsistence frontier farms nestled among rugged upland areas of virgin forest. The smaller islands to the south of Salt Spring were uninhabited. As a dark-skinned race, the Kanakas would not have been out of place there. Among the first successful settlers on the island's north end was a group of blacks who had come from California to escape discrimination shortly before the American Civil War. In fact, the first schoolteacher on Salt Spring was a black man named John C. Jones. Reverend Ebenezer Robson, who visited in 1861, found

> 21 houses on the same number of claims. Four of the houses [are] inhabited by white people and the remainder by colored people. I preached in the house of a colored man in the evening to about 20 persons all colored except three and one of them is married to a colored man.[1]

There was a smaller concentration of white settlers, some with native wives, in the lush Burgoyne Valley on the island's south end, and a seasonal Saanich Indian encampment at Fulford Harbour. According to one pioneer's account,

> At that time there were no roads, just animal trails. Deer, Wolves and Cougar. A boat to Victoria passed the Island every six weeks or so,

blew her whistle from time to time and the settlers interested paddled out to meet her in canoes. Most of them traded in Victoria, paddled the 120 miles [*sic*] round trip in their canoes.

It was a remote community, but one with many natural advantages:

> Cabins were built of fir logs, roofed with shingles of cedar, and chinked with moss or clay. Most had a fireplace, and [were] lighted by candles made by themselves. . . . Game was plentiful and the woods lush with peavine. The adjoining Sea teemed with fish, its shores with Clams, its bosom with Ducks and Geese, and in their snug one, two and three room cabins, these early pioneers were tolerably comfortable and happy.[2]

Most of the early settlers on Salt Spring pre-empted fertile valley land, which in many cases was far from the sea. This was no great disadvantage because, although they chose to live on an island, the first homesteaders were farmers, not seafarers. They devoted themselves to raising cattle and sheep, planting orchards, and growing vegetables for their own use. Inland sites were also safer from Indian attacks, which took the lives of several settlers in the 1860s. By the mid-1870s, however, the time of the main Kanaka influx, this danger had largely abated.

As befitted a people known for their skills on the water, most Kanakas built their cabins right on the shore. And, although the first generation had to concentrate on clearing land and raising their own food, later generations earned their livelihood increasingly from the sea. They clustered on the two southern ends of Salt Spring—the Isabella Point and Beaver Point areas, which were separated by the waters of Fulford Harbour—and on nearby Russell, Portland, Coal, and (perhaps) Piers islands. All these early homesteads were within easy paddling distance of each other by canoe, the main means of transportation.

The first Kanaka who formally claimed land on Salt Spring Island was named Kiave (also called Kaiwe and Chowy). In early 1868 he pre-empted 150 acres along the shore of Fulford Harbour about halfway between Isabella Point and the head of the harbour. Although by that time there was already a handful of other settler families on Salt Spring's south end, none was nearer than a mile or two away. Kiave was around fifty-seven years old at the time, and had an Indian wife named Mary and an infant daughter, Lucy. In the mid-1870s they also had a baby boy named Frank.

Considering Kiave's age, the size of the trees that grew along that shore, and the lack of power tools, he and his wife performed an amazing feat. In one year they cleared six acres of land, erected seven-foot-high fences and built a house. In early 1869 he applied for a government survey and certificate of improvement. Most likely he was illiterate. His application was written for him, signed, and vouched for by the Hawaiian consul in Victoria, Henry Rhodes, who noted that Kiave "has a good house, a wife and family."[3]

Kiave died in the early 1880s, whereupon his widow married a Songhees Indian and perhaps moved away. In 1885 she became involved in a legal dispute with another Kanaka (apparently William Naukana) and a "Boston Man" (that is, an American) named John Gray over the land on Salt Spring and appealed for help from a justice of the peace. A letter of support, written for her by the former HBC chief factor in Victoria, William Tolmie, described the land as

> three or four acres, cleared and long cultivated by her deceased husband . . . in the midst of a Kanaka or Sandwich Islander settlement. . . . She says the neighboring Kanaka settlers can prove that the land in dispute belonged to Kiave by right of improvement and occupancy, and she desires from your Honor . . . [a] certificate enabling her to lease the land to someone, until her boy, son of Kiave, grows up.[4]

The final disposition of the case is not clear, but Naukana did move from nearby Portland Island to the Isabella Point area of Salt Spring around the mid-1880s.

❋ ❋ ❋

No other Hawaiians pre-empted land on Salt Spring until after the 1872 San Juan settlement. In 1874 William Haumea became the first Kanaka to be registered on the voter's list for Salt Spring Island. Haumea was in his fifties or sixties at the time, and had an Indian wife named Mary and a teenaged daughter of the same name. He is not listed in the HBC records but seems to have had a brother who spent time in the San Juan Islands (see Epilogue).

Haumea and his family settled near Eleanor Point on Salt Spring's southern shore and planted orchards that still bear fruit today. A neighbour recalled that Haumea "had such lovely fruit, we bought all our fruit, eggs and other things from him . . . until we got our own."[5] He must have explored tiny Russell Island, which lay just offshore, and found it attractive, for he acquired a crown grant for Russell Island in 1886 and may have planted an orchard there as well.

The Haumeas' daughter Mary married a Hawaiian-born man called John "Peavine" Kahou (also Kahow or Kahon). In 1883 Kahou pre-empted land not far from the Haumeas and built a comfortable log cabin, which is still occupied, in what is today Ruckle Provincial Park. Kahou and his wife cleared land for a farm and had a son named Isaac William. According to a locally told story, Kahou had a violent temper. While his wife was pregnant a second time with twins, he beat her. Possibly as a result of the beating, she died in childbirth, as did both babies. During the funeral or wake, which was held in the orchard at the Haumeas' house, thunder and lightning struck terror in those assembled, and the house was considered haunted from that time on. Years later, children still refused to walk near it. What is certain is that Mary Kahou died in 1892 and was buried at St. Paul's Catholic church in Fulford Harbour. Her husband sold the house and land that same year and moved away.

Another Kanaka who settled on Salt Spring Island in 1874 was William Nawana (also known as Nuana, Onawon, and other variations.) He pre-empted land at the very tip of Isabella Point. Like William Haumea, Nawana was a Roman Catholic in his fifties with an Indian wife named Mary. At the time, Nawana already had at least four children and fathered at least two more. It is not clear whether he was related to the Joe Nuanna who was hanged for the murders on San Juan Island in 1873 (see Chapter 10). It is unlikely that he was the father of the teenager, as he had a younger son of his own named Joe, who was sixteen at the time of the 1881 census. But he seems to have spent time on San Juan Island, where his daughter Mary (who lived on Salt Spring to the age of ninety-four) was born in 1864. Nawana was still living on Salt Spring in 1897. Because of a name change, his descendants were known by the surnames Tahouney and Kahana.

1875 saw the arrival in the Gulf Islands of William Naukana, the most noted of British Columbia's Kanakas, and the only one who has been deemed

William Naukana.
(BCARS G-65)

worthy of a profile in the *Dictionary of Canadian Biography*. A
tall, wiry, and bearded man,
Naukana (also known as
Naukanna, Nanton, Manton,
Nowkin, Likameen, Lagamin,
Lackaman, and La-Gamine) is
believed to have been of royal
Hawaiian lineage and may have
been the son or nephew of Naukane,
alias John Coxe, who arrived at Astoria
in 1811. He joined the HBC in 1845 and
served a total of ten years at Fort Vancouver, New
Caledonia, Thompson's River, Fort Langley, and Fort Victoria before leaving company service in 1855 or 1856.

When he was old, Naukana regaled his children and grandchildren
with tales of long and harrowing fur-hunting expeditions through unsurveyed
territory. In one darkly comical episode, his group of men was caught by a
sudden snowstorm. Forced to camp, they killed a horse for meat, but most
of the other horses wandered off. When frostbite and hunger drove them
mad, they began thinking about which one of them would become the next
meal. Naukana, the only nonwhite in the bunch, thought he was most likely
to be chosen—so he ran away into the fading light of dusk. Hoping to find
grubs to eat, he dug into the snow with his knife and struck a solid mound.
It was a dead horse, and he quickly hacked off a chunk.

> Armed with the frozen meat, Naukana almost caused hysterics when
> he suddenly stumbled into the firelight out of the dark, holding his
> peace offering. Tears, laughter, all the emotions of men under stress
> bubbled over in hilarious abandonment as the men hardly waited for
> the meat to thaw over the hot fire before they tore into it with their
> teeth.[6]

After his stint with the HBC, Naukana is said to have returned to
Hawaii. He found, however, that his family's land had become a sugar plan-

John Palua Sr.
(BCARS C-2691)

tation and his kin were bitterly divided between Catholics and Protestants. He then assembled a group that returned to the Northwest Coast, settled on San Juan Island, and moved over the border to the Gulf Islands after the 1872 agreement awarded San Juan to the United States. All that is documented of that time is that, after leaving HBC service, Naukana was in the Puget Sound area in 1865 (see Chapter 9 for his letter home) and farmed on San Juan Island in 1870 or 1871.

In August 1875 Naukana and his partner John Palua pre-empted most of Portland Island. In addition to farming, they may have operated a water-taxi service, using a canoe to haul people and freight among the islands. They raised sheep and cattle, planted fruit trees, and had large vegetable gardens. Naukana also grew his own tobacco, which he would stuff into a hollow log, adding a bit of rum and allowing it to cure. When it was ready, he would saw off a piece of the log and enjoy a smoke or chew. When he moved from San Juan Island he brought with him favourite varieties of apple trees and raspberry canes, and even a white rose bush that still thrived many decades later.

Introducing cattle to Portland Island, where there were no wharves, was not quite so easy. They had to be brought in close to shore by steamer, pushed overboard, and forced to swim ashore. In all, Naukana and Palua cleared some eighty to one hundred acres of land. They cut down the trees with axes and saws, used oxen to pull the stumps, and burned the debris. This must have taken years of gruelling work. Today, the flat, wooded island, which lies about two miles south of Salt Spring, is also known as Princess Margaret Marine Park and is a very popular destination for boaters. Its orchards and remaining fields are kept trimmed by a flock of feral sheep that have survived there since the island was last farmed several decades ago. In honour of its first settlers, there is a well-marked Kanaka

The Tahouney house on Isabella Point.
(Salt Spring Island Hist. Soc.)

Trail that leads to Kanaka Bluff. Offshore are the tiny Pellow Islets, named for John Palua, who was also sometimes called Johnny Pallow.

Naukana and his wife, whose name is unknown, had at least six daughters, two of whom married fellow Kanakas or part Kanakas, and possibly a son, who is thought to have drowned at the age of fourteen while on a fishing trip to the Fraser River. On Portland Island they built a large house, which became a social centre for the area's growing Kanaka community. In 1885 the first school on Salt Spring's south end was built at Beaver Point. At first, the children from Portland Island rowed across two miles of open water to get there and back each day. But they missed many days of schooling due to bad weather, so Naukana moved to Salt Spring with his youngest daughter, Matilda. He held on to his Portland Island property, however, until shortly before his death in 1909.

John Palua was already married to Naukana's daughter Sophie when they settled on Portland Island. Hawaiian-born and in his late fifties when he arrived on the island, he was a big, heavily built man with the strength needed to clear land. He arrived in British Columbia around 1859 and became a naturalized Canadian in 1889. Most likely, then, it was between 1857 and 1859 that Naukana went home to Hawaii and returned with

The Peavine cabin, built in the 1880s.
(Salt Spring Island Hist. Soc.)

his group of friends and relatives (John Palua among them) to gold-rush-era Victoria and then to San Juan Island. Palua and Sophie had at least five children, including a son named John Palua Jr., who is documented as born in "British Columbia" in 1865. San Juan Island was considered part of the province at that time.

Living with William Naukana and John Palua on Portland Island was a Hawaiian named Thomas Tamaree (also known as Thomas Komaree). He was probably the Thomas Tamaree who worked for the HBC as late as 1860, served with the Victoria Voltigeurs (see Chapter 8), and was Kanaka Pete's friend Tamalee in Nanaimo in 1868 (see Chapter 10). Although he was around the same age as Naukana and Palua, Tamaree does not seem to have pre-empted land on Portland Island. Unlike the other men, in one census he was listed as a labourer rather than a farmer. Presumably, he worked for one or both of them, even though he was the only one who could read or write. He remained part of the large Palua household at least until 1893.

❋   ❋   ❋

On Coal Island, which lies between Portland Island and the Saanich Peninsula, there were two Kanaka families, the Kamais and the Carneys. Kama Kamai, the first Coal Island settler, had an Indian wife named Mary and at least six children. He seems to have lived on San Juan Island and worked there as a boatman during the period of the Pig War. An "indigent Kanaka named Kami" from San Juan Island was briefly held in the case of teen-aged murderer Joe Nuanna in 1873. Perhaps this was a son of Kamai who stayed behind. Kama Kamai pre-empted 160 acres on Coal Island in 1873 and passed his holding on to his son Louis Kamai in 1884. Louis did not stay on Coal Island, but moved to Victoria, where he lived with a baker and his family and became a baker himself.

Less is known for certain about the Carney family, who shared Coal Island with the Kamais. There is a Carney Point on the island's northern side, just as there is a Kamai Point on the southeastern tip. Alexander Carney farmed there in 1891, when he was forty years old, but his background is unclear. He may have been born in North America to parents who were both Hawaiian-born, which, if true, would be quite unusual. His wife Mary, whom he married in 1870, may have had a Hawaiian-born father, but another source lists her as a Songhees Indian. The Carneys had at least four children.

*Jenny Kahana-nui and
her children.*
(Salt Spring Island Hist. Soc.)

Several other native-born Hawaiians settled in the Gulf Islands, but
the information on them is even more sketchy. A Kanaka named Kanalio
farmed on Salt Spring in 1881 with his Indian wife, Mary. George Napoleon Parker, said to be Hawaiian-born, married Naukana's daughter Cecile
and farmed on northern Salt Spring in today's town of Ganges, some ten
miles from the main concentration of Kanakas. Also in the Ganges area
was a Kanaka family named Kahana-Nui. They may have been related to
the HBC servant Kahannui, who worked at Fort Nisqually in the 1840s and
early 1850s and left the company in 1854 or 1855.

A man named Henry Mundon lived on Salt Spring's Isabella Point.
He is said to have gone to Washington, D.C. at one point to lobby the United
States government to retain the Hawaiian monarchy. He was still living on
Salt Spring in 1897. Also on Isabella Point was the shy Kanaka named Kea
who mistook the teacher Cooke for a descendant of Captain Cook (see
Chapter 3). This may have been the Kea who worked for the HBC at Fort
Langley in the early to mid-1850s and at Victoria as late as 1859–60. And
on Beaver Point there was a "Kanaka Bill," who may have squatted on the
land that is now Ruckle Provincial Park. There is also mention of a Kanaka
family on Piers Island, near the Saanich Peninsula, though the name is unknown.

In all, the first generation of Kanakas who settled in the Gulf Islands
appears to have numbered over a dozen households. There may well have
been other individuals who squatted in the little Hawaiian community or
otherwise escaped notice in official records and the memories of Kanaka
descendants.

15

Toe-Tickling Luaus

he Gulf Islands Kanaka community reached its greatest size around the 1890s. This was the period when the elderly full-blooded Hawaiian men (Naukana, Palua, Haumea, and Nawana) were still alive and their children had married and begun to raise families of their own. Then, early this century, the last of the original Kanakas passed on and many of the second- and third-generation families began to move away, in many cases to steadier jobs and more comfortable lives than was offered by subsistence farming and fishing in the Gulf Islands. At its peak, however, the little colony centred on Salt Spring Island amounted to at least two dozen Kanaka or part-Kanaka households.

Even two dozen households may give a conservative impression of the number of people in this community. In an era that knew only crude methods of contraception and high rates of infant mortality, early settlers on the coast tended to have large families. The Kanakas were no exception. Naukana's youngest daughter, Matilda, for example, had six children by her first husband, James Harris, then nine more by her second, Peter George Roland. Maria Mahoy, whose life story is related in Chapter 16, had at least twelve children by two successive husbands.

Not surprisingly, there was much intermarriage among the Kanakas and part Kanakas. Even the rather incomplete family histories that are available reveal at least seven such marriages. These relationships both reflected the natural sense of community that existed within the tightly knit Gulf Islands settlement and helped, in turn, to reinforce the Kanaka identity. Of course, the barriers of island geography and race also made it difficult to meet alternative partners.

Class photo, Isabella Point School, 1905. Willy Palua (left) holds the scroll of honour. (Salt Spring Island Archives)

Considering these enduring familial ties, it is interesting that the Hawaiian language was not, in most cases, passed on to the second and third generations. To Naukana descendant Paul Roland, it was mainly a matter of transferred allegiance: "Those first Hawaiian settlers were so loyal to the men who brought them here that they said, 'Never mind the old language,' and forbade the children to speak it."[1] Nawana descendant Jackie (Lumley) Hembruff recalls, however, that her Aunt Grace, who was part Kanaka on both sides of her family, wanted to teach her Hawaiian, but she—at the time only a child—did not want to learn it. Jackie Hembruff's mother, American-born Becky (Carpenter) Lumley, also spoke Hawaiian as a child, but lost the language in adulthood. "The U.S. government allowed nothing but English,"[2] she recalled, at the Indian school near Salem, Oregon, which she attended from about 1917 to 1920. The Kanakas of Isabella Point had a big, ancient Hawaiian-language Bible, in which they recorded their marriages, births, and deaths. Unfortunately, it was destroyed in a house fire in 1943.

Some Hawaiian traditions were passed along, however. Paul Roland's mother told him legends of Hawaiian deities and about the power of the *kahunas,* or traditional sorcerers. The *hukilau* method of fishing was also practised along the beaches of Isabella Point. In this technique, men drag a long seine net out into the water and form a semicircle, while others beat the water with tree branches to drive the fish into the net. In fact, this is not very different from a smelt-fishing method used by Northwest Coast Indians. A few Kanaka families also remained partial to *poi,* a dish made from the baked, pounded, moistened, and fermented root of the taro plant.

The most colourful Hawaiian tradition that survived in the Gulf Islands was the luau. When the harvest was over and the cold and wet season set in, the entire community would gather for a series of these moveable feasts. Whether all the formalities continued to be observed—including the verandah-like lanai—is unclear. The key features of these Gulf Islands luaus were the outdoor cooking—in a firepit dug into the beach—and the unshackled revelry.

The homemade liquor flowed and the music rang, recalled William Naukana's grandson Paul Roland:

> There were such big crowds that some danced all day and some slept all day. The ones that slept all day, they danced all night. Then they'd move over to Coal Island, to the Kamais' and Carneys'. Then to Piers Island. I've forgotten the Hawaiian name—and they'd dance there for a week. They'd come up to Portland Island, to Grandpa's place, and dance there for a week. Then come over to Salt Spring here to Palua's and dance there for a week, and to Kahana's down at Isabella Pt. . . . They sang and danced all winter, until the time came to put in their crops.[3]

On Salt Spring, their non-Kanaka neighbours were often included. Bea Hamilton, who lived next door to a Kanaka family, wrote,

> It has been said that one taste of [the] home brew and things would begin to whoop as one of the biggest guitar-twanging, toe-tickling luaus got under way. Here the party would gather speed day by day and many a group could out-wiggle any Hawaiian affair ever staged in their native land. There are still chuckles when the descendants talk of the time when old Nawana was given a shot of whisky and danced the big Norwegian, Johnny Sparrow, off his feet. Long after Johnny had collapsed from sheer exhaustion, Old Nawana was still doing a lively tap dance.[4]

Hamilton fondly recalled teaching the ukulele to Kanaka children and how one little girl, named Mary Ellen, wore a cook's hat and did a Highland fling in a school concert. Hamilton's sister, Mabel Davis, had a very romantic memory of the Hawaiians, who worked the beaches at night by the twinkle of hurricane lanterns. They were very musical, she recalled:

> Some of them could yodel. You can imagine how nice that sounded on a clear evening—yodelling, the sounds coming over the water. They'd go out and dig clams, and you would hear them singing while they dug. . . . It sounded awfully nice in the moonlight.[5]

She, too, remembered the Kanakas singing and playing string instruments at school concerts and as very fine step-dancers.

Clams, fish, deer, and other rich resources from sea and forest meant that there was never a shortage of food. Naukana grandson Jack Roland recalled the great abundance of salmon and herring along Isabella Point during his youth:

> When [the herring] came in to spawn, they came in by the tons. You could walk in up to your knees in spawn . . . The wind would wash it up onto the beach. I've seen this harbour just like a big milk pond. . . . Crabbing was [also] very popular at that time.[6]

Most of the Kanakas also planted fruit trees, as did nearly all the early settlers. Apple growing was so successful that Salt Spring Island became a major supplier to the markets of Victoria and Vancouver. Berries also grew wild in such profusion that Saanich and Cowichan Indians continued to come to Salt Spring to pick berries, as they had long before the first settlers.

Daily routine for the Kanaka settlers involved dawn-to-dusk manual labour. For the men, there was hunting and fishing, hauling water, tending the livestock, plowing, cutting hay, and cutting huge piles of firewood. For the women, it was endless cooking, laundry, dishes, and other household chores, working in the garden, putting up food, making clothes, and raising the children. But for all the hard work and lack of modern medicine, it was a healthy existence. Although they ate copious amounts of foods that are considered questionable today—red meat, butter, whole milk, eggs, oysters—they do not seem to have suffered many heart attacks. Perhaps the steady, vigorous work meant that they burnt off excess calories and fats. The water and air and food were pure, the environment relatively free of parasites, and the temperate climate benign. And aside from the considerable dangers of boating or logging accidents, it was a relatively safe and low-stress way of life. Many of the first-generation Kanakas lived an impressively long time, even by today's standards: William Naukana died at ninety-six; John Palua at ninety; William Haumea in his late eighties; Maria Mahoy at eighty-six; Mary Nawana in her early nineties.

Despite this longevity, in the first decade of the twentieth century the Kanaka community saw the passing of the Hawaiian-born settlers. William Haumea died in 1902. John Palua died in 1907. William Naukana sold his Portland Island property in 1907 and died on Salt Spring in 1909. He was buried at St. Paul's Catholic Church on Fulford Harbour, which he had helped to build. His obituary noted,

> Ever ready to oblige a friend or forgive a foe, this last of the Kanakas is leaving behind him a reputation for honesty and square dealing which many a white man would envy. Likameen [a nickname] was industrious and active until only a few days before his death.[7]

❋ ❋ ❋

Although some left, many second-generation Kanakas and their families remained in the Gulf Islands. John Pallow, the son of John Palua, worked at logging and had at least five children by two successive wives. Several of Naukana's daughters stayed on Salt Spring Island with their families: Sophie with John Palua Sr. and their children; Matilda with her first husband, James Harris, and then her second, Peter George Roland; Julia with George Shepherd (they had at least two children, one of whom, William, spent the rest of his life on the island).

Mary Ann and Lewis Peterson, a Danish-born fisherman, lived on Isabella Point but both died in 1903 while still quite young. William Nawana's daughter Mary married William Lumley and raised twelve children at Isabella Point. One of their sons, Ed Lumley, married part-Kanaka Becky Carpenter and raised one of the Kanaka families that is still on Salt Spring to this day.

Other Nawana offspring who stayed on Salt Spring with their own families for many years were Joseph Tahouney and John Kahano. On sparsely populated Saturna Island in the 1890s, Dutch-born John Wessell had a wife named Agnes, whose father was Hawaiian-born.

Other first-generation Kanakas and their offspring eventually moved away from Salt Spring. John Peavine Kahou left after the death of his wife in 1892 (see Chapter 14). George Napoleon Parker, with his wife Cecile and their children, left by 1899 to work as a fisherman on Bowen Island in Howe Sound. Maria Mahoy's oldest son, George Douglas, moved with his wife to fish and homestead on Lasqueti Island in 1911 (see Chapter 16). Others, such as William Nawana's grandson, Ed Lumley, and Maria Mahoy's son, Abel Douglas Jr., spent much of their working lives away from the Gulf Islands as loggers or fishermen but retained close ties to the Kanaka community and returned in their later years.

The subsistence homesteads remained, but increasingly the opportunities were in fishing and logging. These were largely seasonal jobs, which brought in needed hard cash. Around the turn of the century, "going fishing" sometimes meant long, dangerous trips to the Bering Sea or the coast of California to hunt seals. The details are sketchy, but on one of these trips in 1904, the schooner *Triumph,* carrying a group of Salt Spring men, including some Kanaka descendants, was wrecked and all the men drowned.

The Lumley family, circa 1910. Standing from left: William Lumley Jr., William Lumley Sr., Mary (Nawana) Lumley, Richard Lumley, Robert Lumley. Younger children are not identified. (Salt Spring Island Hist. Soc.)

By the First World War the seal hunt was defunct but salmon fishing was at its peak, and many men combined it with farming. Willy Palua, for example, was both a fisherman and a farmer. So were Ernie Fisher and Abel Douglas Jr., the sons of Maria Mahoy on Russell Island. Ed Lumley used to go up to the Skeena River with his gillnetter to fish with Abel Douglas and other local men under contract to the big fish companies. Later, Ed Lumley became a tugboat captain. By the 1920s and 1930s, nearly all the male Kanaka descendants went to the Fraser River in the summer to fish for the big canneries: "Most of them had sailboats, big skiffs with sails on them and manpower. And an old one-lunger Easthope engine—if they were lucky enough."[8]

Logging and sawmill work were dangerous ways to earn cash, but often they had the advantage of being closer to home. Peter Roland, Matilda Naukana's second husband, sometimes worked as a commercial fisherman, sometimes as a logger. By 1912 there was a log yarding and booming ground along the Isabella Point shore, including a dangerous steel cable system that local residents had to be very careful to avoid. In the early 1920s at least half a dozen portable mills were established on Salt Spring to cut railway ties for the export market. These provided jobs for all the able-bodied men who wanted them. A much larger sawmill was established at Cusheon Cove in the Beaver Point area between 1906 and 1908, and operated until its wharf collapsed in the late 1920s. Peter Roland and his oldest son sometimes worked at the Cusheon Cove sawmill and lived there in the bunkhouse. Younger son Jack Roland recalled that he used to visit them once a week—it was a long walk—and bring them food.

> Myself, I started logging in the summertime when school was out, pulling the old Swede fiddle, as they called it in those days—the hand saw—with my Dad. During the 30s I went logging in Alberni. At that time, it was still all hand falling.[9]

Only after the war did power saws come into use.

Modern conveniences were slow to come to the Kanaka community. In the late 1930s there was only one car on Isabella Point. Heating and cooking continued to be by wood stoves. Outhouses were still the rule, indoor plumbing the exception. And most transportation was still by water. It was much easier to hop into a canoe and paddle up Fulford Harbour to the store and post office than to hitch up a horse or hike along trails and dirt

S.S. Iroquois *at Fulford Harbour, 1905.*
(Salt Spring Island Hist. Soc.)

roads and carry everything home in a backpack. Horses and carriages were used on Sundays, however, to attend services at St. Paul's Church at the head of Fulford Harbour.

From 1885 to 1904, most Kanaka children attended school at Beaver Point, which, for those on Isabella Point, also entailed a trip by canoe or rowboat and then a hike. The one-room Isabella Point school opened in 1904. In the early years, most of the pupils were Kanaka offspring. A graduation photo (circa 1905) shows a proud Willy Palua holding the valedictorian's scroll.

❋ ❋ ❋

With successive generations, the Kanaka community in the Gulf Islands gradually lost its cohesiveness. Kanaka descendants married non-Kanakas, often moved away, and in any case melded into the mainstream of economic and social life. Although they remained aware of their unusual backgrounds, the memories and traditions of their parents and grandparents were less and less relevant. The Hawaiian heritage on Salt Spring and nearby islands seemed doomed to be forgotten.

Then, in the early 1970s, the jet age arrived. A visiting Hawaiian journalist named Mary Cooke heard about the Hawaiian colony on Salt Spring. She met and interviewed Paul Roland, who had been confined to a wheelchair for many years and had used his free time to dig into his family's Kanaka past and re-establish contact with distant relatives. Cooke's newspaper, the *Honolulu Advertiser,* joined Canadian Pacific Airlines to invite Paul, his sister Sophie Tahouney, and nephew John Roland for a gala, expenses-paid trip to Hawaii. They were greeted at the airport by an elaborate procession and by members of the George C. Naukana family. The discovery of a lost Hawaiian colony in Canada was a headline event in Honolulu. Wined and dined at every turn, they met with historians and genealogists and came home more eager than ever to tell their story.

The hoopla also revived interest in the Kanakas on Salt Spring itself. One result was a chapter devoted to the Kanakas in Bea Hamilton's highly anecdotal history of Salt Spring Island. Since that first visit, others in the Roland family have gone to Hawaii. So has Nawana descendant Jackie Hembruff, who in the late 1970s opened a restaurant on Salt Spring called the Kanaka Place.

The Rolands decided to revive the luau feasts as colourful events to which the entire south Salt Spring community was invited, both for fun and to raise money for local athletics. Jack Roland and his sons would prepare the *imu,* or firepit, by digging a big pit in the beach, lining it with rocks, and building a bonfire until the rocks were white hot. "Next," Jack's widow Laura recalls,

> he would scoop out the wood, cover the rocks with green seaweed and put in the food, all wrapped of course. Clams, oysters, salmon, meat. Then he'd cover it with more seaweed, put a big carpet or tarp over it and let it cook for hours. It was a winner![10]

These luaus were held at intervals throughout the 1970s, but petered out after Jack Roland's death.

Today, there are quite a few Kanaka descendants on Salt Spring Island. Some still have distinctly Hawaiian physical features. As Paul Roland once said, "The Hawaiian blood is very strong."[11] But the only conspicuous signs of the Kanaka heritage are street names (Roland Road and Kanaka Road) and the Kanaka Restaurant in Ganges. And there is the little graveyard at St. Paul's Church, with its expansive view of Isabella Point and the gravestones of the Paluas, the Tahouneys, the Haumeas' daughter Mary, and old William Naukana, whose much-abused surname is given, inexplicably, as Nowkin.

16

Whistle for the Wind

A n orchard is a living monument to the person who plants it. As noted in the introduction, it was the author's curiosity about the orchard on Russell Island that, as much as any other single inspiration, led to this book. Russell Island is a fitting place to begin and end a history of Kanakas on the Northwest Coast. For the story behind those gnarled old apple trees and the people who took care of them neatly encapsulates nearly every theme in the saga of the Hawaiian settlement in British Columbia and the Pacific Northwest.

Russell Island's forty acres of rock and forest form a long, flattened S that lies one-half mile off, and roughly parallel to, the southern shore of Salt Spring Island on the eastern (Beaver Point) side of Fulford Harbour. The southern side of Russell Island is exposed to the blasts of winter southeasterlies; its clifftops are dotted with swept-back pines, arbutus, and Garry oaks. The northern side of the island is sheltered from all but the worst northwesterlies and provides a good spot for a wharf and reasonable anchorage. In anything but the fiercest storms, the island creates a leeward windshadow that allows small boats to be launched safely and rowed across to Salt Spring. This permitted the young Fisher children who lived there to go to Beaver Point school.

As was related earlier, William Haumea settled on Salt Spring by 1874 and established orchards not far from the sea on land facing Russell Island. Exactly when he first explored the small island is not known, but by 1886 he owned it. His descendants are not certain whether Haumea himself cleared the huge Douglas firs and planted the first fruit trees. In 1902 Haumea died and left the island to Maria Mahoy, who owned it until her death in 1936

Maria (Mahoy) Douglas at the age of thirty. (Karey Litton)

and whose family retained ownership and lived there until 1960. One old-time Salt Spring resident believed that Maria had looked after Haumea in his declining years. In some accounts, he had legally adopted her. When Haumea made out his will and left all his property to Maria, he referred to her as Mary Ann Haumea.

The origins of Maria Mahoy (also Mahoi and Mahoya) are maddeningly obscure. She was born around 1857, probably in Esquimalt, to a father named William Mahoya and an unknown mother who is thought to have died at her birth. Maria's father was probably the HBC servant Bill Mahoy, who was engaged in Oahu on August tenth, 1837 and served first at Fort Vancouver and then at the Willamette Valley Sawmill. In August 1846, after nine years in HBC service, he returned to Hawaii. In July 1848, he apparently signed up again with the HBC and returned to the Northwest Coast to work as a labourer on the steamship *Beaver*. A few years later he may have been transferred to the schooner *Cadboro,* though he is also listed as a midman at Fort Rupert. His last employment with the HBC was probably in Victoria in 1853–54. He seems to have been living on Salt Spring Island at the time of his death in 1881.

Maria's grandchildren recall her using the name Mahoya-Kamahehe, which may provide a clue to her origins on her mother's side. It is likely, given the marriage patterns of HBC servants on the Northwest Coast, that her mother was either a native Indian, or half-Hawaiian and half-Indian, which could account for the tag-on name Kamahehe. There was an HBC servant named Kamakeha who served eight years, first at Fort McLoughlin and then at Fort Victoria, before returning to Hawaii in 1847. He came back to the HBC in 1848 and worked mainly at Fort Victoria until his death there in 1854–55. Perhaps Maria's mother was the child of an early liaison (around 1840) between Kamakeha and an Indian woman.

Whatever her origins, by 1871, when she was only fourteen or fifteen, Maria's slim figure and finely etched features must have caught the
attention of a young American whaling captain named Abel Douglas—
sometimes spelled Douglass. Maria was soon pregnant with the first of her
many children, a son named George Douglas.

Born in Maine, at the age of twenty-seven Abel Douglas was recruited
in San Francisco by James Dawson of Victoria to be skipper of British
Columbia's first commercially successful whaling ship, the small forty-
seven-ton schooner *Kate*. They began hunting marine leviathans in August
1868, killing eight whales in Saanich Inlet and rendering them into oil at a
nearby base on shore. By the end of the first season they had sold about one
hundred barrels of humpback oil. The following year the Dawson and
Douglass Whaling Company established a base farther north in the Strait
of Georgia, at Cortes Island, where the main settlement is still called
Whaletown. In 1871 Douglas went into business with a different partner,
sailing a scow-schooner with the less-than-romantic name *Industry*.

Shipwrecks, the pillaging of beached whales by natives, and declining prices for whale oil soon led to the temporary collapse of commercial
whaling on British Columbia's inner coast. Douglas switched to building
and sailing schooners as part of Victoria's large seal-hunting fleet. He joined
American and Russian ships in the lucrative slaughter of fur seals in the
Bering Sea and Pribilof Islands. His ships included the highly successful
schooner *Triumph* (not the *Triumph* that sank in 1904; see Chapter 15) and
then the *Challenge,* which, along with many other Victoria ships, was seized
by the Americans in 1888 for allegedly hunting in American waters. (His
descendants say that he was eventually compensated for part of his loss.)
He also occasionally ran freight between Victoria and New Westminster
and chartered his schooner to government surveyors and scientists.

Douglas returned to whaling on the inner coast in the late 1880s, towing the carcasses to a shore site on Pasley Island in Howe Sound, where he
had sheds and giant pots to render the blubber. One Vancouver old-timer
recalled seeing him working his ship with his two young sons, George and
Alfred, on board.

The years when her husband was away at sea for long stretches must
have been trying ones for Captain Douglas's young wife with her six children. They lived in the Beaver Point area of Salt Spring, not far from William Haumea, and were prosperous enough to have a young Indian house
servant, which was quite unusual at the time. By the late 1880s, however,

the marriage had failed. Douglas, who was sailing the schooner *Arietas* out of Victoria as late as 1893, disappeared from Maria's life. He apparently continued to live in Victoria until 1906 and then moved to Seattle, where he died in 1908 at the age of sixty-seven or sixty-eight. Maria, who was still an attractive woman in her early thirties, consummated an affair with a man nearly ten years her junior. George Fisher accepted responsibility for her previous children and stayed with her for the remaining nearly half-century of her life.

❋　❋　❋

Fisher was born in 1865 on Piers Island, near today's Swartz Bay ferry terminal, to a well-to-do English father, Edward Brant Fisher, and an Indian (probably Cowichan) mother. That same year, Fisher senior was shot to death on the Cowichan reserve. His infant son was sent to Victoria to be raised by Catholic priests and educated at St. Louis College. He remained active in church affairs throughout his life. His mother, Annie Rollestomet, remarried in 1879, this time to a man named George Purser who farmed on Salt Spring's Beaver Point.

Perhaps this geographical connection led to the liaison between Annie's son and Maria Douglas, who was by then a mother with a frequently absent husband. By 1887—about the time Maria had her last Douglas child, Abel William Douglas—Fisher was a neighbour and farmer on Salt Spring's south end. Around 1890, when he was in his mid-twenties, Fisher became the father of the first of Maria's second set of children, Mary Jane Fisher. Maria

Maria (Mahoy) Fisher and daughter Mary Jane Fisher.
(Karey Litton)

not only gave birth at least twelve times herself, she was also valued as a midwife and delivered many babies on Salt Spring Island, including several of her own daughters' children.

When William Haumea died in 1902, Maria inherited Russell Island and moved there. She and George Fisher built the little saltbox-style frame house on the island that is still occupied today. (There is also a large, modern house built in the 1970s by the post-Kanaka owners, John and Elizabeth Rohrer.) They fenced in several acres of pasture near the house and orchard and maintained a small flock of sheep, as well as chickens and a milk cow. They also planted a cash crop of strawberries, which, because of the small island's sunny exposure and particularly mild microclimate, ripened a week or two earlier than others in the area and brought George Fisher a good price when he sold them on Salt Spring. The apples and peaches flourished in the orchard, as did the grapes from the arbour.

George Fisher fished part-time for cash as well as to put food on the table. He and Maria also gathered a type of seaweed called slukas. They dried and sold it to a Chinese cash buyer who came around in his schooner and purchased the delicacy for sale in the Chinatowns of Victoria and Vancouver. George had a little slip on the island's sheltered side, where he could pull his fishing boat up onto shore. He built boats in the barn and may have sold some. He also pruned trees for people on Salt Spring and is remembered by his grandchildren as a jack of all trades, which was unusual for a relatively well-educated man who had been raised in the provincial capital.

To maintain her crowded household, Maria Fisher worked for hours each day at the wood-burning cookstove, preparing meals, boiling clothes and diapers in huge tubs, and scrubbing them by hand on a washboard. She also put up huge quantities of fruits and vegetables. There was no house servant to help, as there had been with Captain Douglas. Living in cash-starved circumstances, she never threw away a bottle, can, or jar. Everything had its use. She made her own canning jars by tying a string (probably soaked in kerosene) around a glass bottle, lighting it, then cracking the bottle along the heated line and filing the edges smooth. In place of metal lids or wax, she sealed the jars with a paste made from flour and water, which was smeared on brown paper cut from old bags and wrapped tightly around the top of the truncated bottles.

The Fishers had no refrigeration, so Maria hung butter and other perishables down the well. Surplus herring and salmon were smoked in the

Wedding dinner of Mary Jane Fisher and W.H. Roberts on Russell Island, circa 1910. (Karey Litton)

small smokehouse. She also dug clams to earn extra cash, and even in her old age could lift a large sackful of clams in each arm. The Fishers adopted the Indian practice of collecting herring spawn on cedar boughs by draping them in the water. They also liked to eat the "roe" (actually the gonads) of sea urchins, which they called "sea eggs" or *squitsi*. They preferred the small green variety to the larger red ones that are taken commercially today by British Columbia's dive fishery.

If other sea food was unavailable and the tide was low, Maria would go down to the far end of the island and spear a big octopus from a subtidal crevice where they congregated. These creatures became part of Russell Island lore. Maria's great-grandchildren, who often spent their summers on the island, liked to dig clams. She warned them, however, not to leave their buckets unattended on the beach. Once, she claimed, she had done so and come back to find a huge octopus running away down the beach—with the bucket of clams tucked under one of its arms. Abel Douglas Jr. warned Maria's grandchildren to watch out for octopus on warm days. The long-tentacled beasts would—so he said—reach into overhanging arbutus branches and hoist themselves up to enjoy a bit of sunshine. Thoroughly spooked, the children never walked along the shore without looking up at the trees first.

Maria and George's children attended the one-room school on Beaver Point, the longest continually operating school in British Columbia. (In the 1970s it was refurbished and has been used in recent years as an alternative school, kindergarten, and preschool by the Beaver Point community.) A former teacher, Elma Rowbotham, recalled "the little Fishers bringing their shy smiles after rowing across from Russell Island,"[1] and the struggle she had in winter to keep the fire going in the wood stove. One of the Fishers' grandchildren, Violet Bell, was delivered by Maria on Russell Island. She later attended the largely Kanaka Isabella Point School, boarding on Salt Spring with her Aunt Ellen (née Douglas) and Uncle Willy Shepherd.

While the Fisher children were growing up on Russell Island, most of the Douglases had reached adulthood and moved away. The oldest boy, George Douglas, born in Victoria in 1871, was tall and athletic. He worked first at sealing with his father and later on the booming grounds at Cowichan Bay. He was particularly nimble in the tricky dance of log-sorters as they hop from one floating log to another with a pike pole in one hand. In 1911, George and his wife Emma moved up the Strait of Georgia to Lasqueti Island, where they joined the earliest homesteaders on a large holding of their own and lived there until the 1950s.

Mary Jane (Fisher) Roberts with husband W.H. Roberts and daughters Gladys and Violet.
(Karey Litton)

Abel Douglas Jr., who was born around 1886, went into logging and fishing. He based his boat for many years in Prince Rupert, never married, and often returned to Russell Island to visit his mother—and have her do his laundry. In the 1950s he returned to the island and lived there alone, until after it had been sold and he was too feeble to stay on his own. Ellen Douglas moved only as far as Salt Spring, where she married Willy Shepherd, whose half-Kanaka mother was William Naukana's daughter, Julia. Willy spent his life at a typical mix of fishing, farming, and logging work. Both George and Abel Douglas Jr. served in Europe during the First World War. So did their half-brother Ernest Fisher, who was too young but ran away and lied about his age. The war took a terrible toll of young Salt Spring Island men, but Maria Mahoy's sons came home unscathed.

Life close to home also had its hazards. Alfred Douglas, born around 1878, was an extremely handsome man who had married the daughter of Salt Spring neighbour John Sparrow and settled on Salt Spring himself. In 1907 he was shot to death by another neighbour, George Williams, after they had been drinking, perhaps during a card game. Williams ran away but was caught eventually and served a long prison term. Maria's grandchildren believe that Williams had been jealous of his wife's attraction to the good-looking Alfred.

Nor was the Douglas murder the only one to occur in that area. Across from Russell Island on Salt Spring was a small Saanich Indian reserve that was home to a man named Charlie and his wife, who had a house and fruit trees. Maria and George Fisher were on friendly terms with them and often baked a cake, rowed across, and visited for tea. In the 1920s the Indian couple was found murdered. The suspicion was that someone had been after a cache of gold they had hidden. Maria Fisher knew where the gold was, found it, and turned it over to the police.

❉ ❉ ❉

Family life on Russell Island incorporated a mix of Kanaka, Indian, and mainstream Anglo-Canadian ways. Maria spoke bits of Hawaiian, taught her children and grandchildren to dance the hula, and explained the meaning of the various hand movements. She liked to go out in her canoe during thunderstorms and to swim in the rain, when, she said, the surface of the sea was a bit warmer than usual. While swimming, she would beat her chest and chant to call her *tamanos*. These, she told her grandchildren, were guardian spirits that one could feel.

Maria (Mahoy) Fisher at the age of eighty.
(Karey Litton)

Her late granddaughter, Violet Bell, recalled being sick one time. Maria took her outside and when hummingbirds gathered she explained to the little girl that these were Violet's *tamanos,* and that they would keep her company. Violet Bell also told of Maria's psychic powers. Once, when she was out in the garden, Maria saw a snake and announced with a distinct lack of enthusiasm that Mrs. Nawana from Salt Spring was about to arrive. Sure enough, the little old woman with her black hat and pinched face soon appeared.

Maria also seems to have been influenced by native Indian beliefs. She would listen to the hoot of owls and say that, depending on the speed of the call, it was either a good sign, or a sign of death. She could also "talk Indian," although whether this was Chinook jargon or a local Coast Salish dialect is not clear. And she was on good terms with the Saanich and Cowichan Indians, who often stopped in at Russell Island on their way back from fishing at Active Pass or the Fraser River. The Indians usually brought her fresh fish and Maria always served them tea. Until her death in 1993, Violet Bell still had the sturdy kitchen table where these amicable visits took place.

The Fishers invited their Salt Spring Island neighbours to big parties that went on for days. "The women would bake, the boats would arrive, and they'd play instruments and sing and jig all night," recalled Violet Bell. "They worked hard, but they played hard, too."[2] Another of Maria's granddaughters, Grace Jensen, played ukulele and piano. Salt Spring neighbour Leon King would play his fiddle. The Fishers had no electricity, but they could listen to records on a wind-up gramophone.

Maria died in 1936, but George Fisher stayed on Russell Island until his death in 1948. Their youngest son, Ernest Fisher, was living in Steveston as a commercial fisherman at the time. He came back to Russell Island for some years after his father's death, but then moved to Prince Rupert. Maria's oldest surviving son, Abel Douglas Jr., returned to Russell Island in the 1950s and lived there until the family sold the island (around 1960) to the Rohrer family of Long Beach, California, for use as a summer retreat. In his mid-seventies at the time, he then moved in with relatives in Victoria, where he died in 1966.

The Kanaka descendants who spent part of their youth on Russell Island still return occasionally for visits and look back on their time there with great fondness. "It was paradise," says the Fishers' grandson, Harry Roberts, who loved to spend his summer vacations there as a child. "The orchard was kept immaculate, with split rail fences all around. They earned a living off that island, with sheep, cows and a commercial crop of early vegetables."[3]

The tenacious pioneer spirit that the Kanakas brought to the British Columbia coast lives on in Roberts's memory of his formidable grandmother. Even as an old woman, he says, Maria Mahoy was an intrepid sailor. When she needed substantial supplies, she would pack the grandchildren into her sixteen-foot clinker centreboarder and sail off to relatively distant Sidney, where the prices were lower than on nearby Salt Spring. In a strong wind she would lean out and heel the boat right over. If the breeze failed, she had only to whistle for a while, and soon her sails filled again. "It was an old Hawaiian superstition," Roberts chuckles, but he swears it worked for her. As her Kanaka ancestors had done before her, "she would whistle for the wind."[4]

Epilogue

ugust 1994. A hot sun beats down on the small beachfront park on Salt Spring Island, where three hundred Kanaka descendants have gathered for a good-time, modern-day luau. Kids wade out into gentle waves and small boats dance at anchor just offshore. Steam wafts from the traditional *imu,* or covered firepit, dug into the sand. It is filled with clams, mussels, and oysters, and covered with thick layers of seaweed and burlap. A whole pig rotates on a spit over a wood fire. The occasion is the third annual reunion of Kanaka descendants and the island's first major luau in at least two decades.

Larry Bell, of Abbotsford, B.C., the master of ceremonies, kicks off the festivities: "Aloha." Introduce yourselves to those sitting near you, he says. "I've found a bunch of relations I didn't even know existed." Then he tells about a recent trip to Hawaii, his first to his ancestral homeland.

> We were at a heiau—a temple, with lava rocks and pieces of ti leaves. I sat down with my wife and said to her, "Can't you feel it? Can't you feel something happening here?" And I started to cry.

Bell's half-brother, Karey Litton, says a brief prayer

> to the Great Spirit, to God the Father. He gave our ancestors a very beautiful land to live in. And they did go forth and they did multiply. We can be very grateful for these beautiful islands. The Gulf Islands. The San Juan Islands. And for our forefathers, our ancestors, for what they went through—the hard times—but still they prospered.

Larry Bell introduces Don Watt and Tony Farr of the Salt Spring Island Historical Society, who have brought along a bronze plaque (since installed at St. Paul's Roman Catholic Church) giving a brief history of the Kanakas on Salt Spring and the Gulf Islands. This is the first success Bell has had in several years of lobbying local governments, museums, and other organizations to acknowledge formally the existence and contribution of his ancestors. He says a few words reminding everyone of the close familial ties between the Kanakas and the Indian peoples of the Northwest Coast.

Roland family singing Hawaiian songs. From left: Cathy Roland, Dave Roland, Lou Roland, Leona Cook, Josephine Morrison.
(Tom Koppel)

"We're all one people, all one blood." And he introduces visiting native dance groups.

To the throb of skin drums, the Khowutzun Tzinquaw dancers, Cowichan Indians from nearby Duncan on Vancouver Island, perform a series of dances evoking paddling, the search for spiritual guidance, and individual friendship. Pauline Hillaire, from the Lummi Reservation in Washington State, drums and chants, while boys from Lummi dance wear-

Natasha Johnston does a Tahitian drum dance.
(Tom Koppel)

Boy from Lummi Reservation, Washington, dances at luau.
(Tom Koppel)

ing carved wooden wolf masks and real bearskins. Hillaire is part Hawaiian herself, the descendant of Henry Haumea, who landed from a sailing ship in the San Juan Islands and moved to the Lummi Reservation near Bellingham in 1855. "The Hawaiians brought along a game called Jumping Sticks, but now the Lummi own it," she chuckles. "I'm only one-eighth Hawaiian, but it still shows. In my family, we're all big—my father has giant hands—and we all have curly hair here, right behind the ears. We stand out from others at Lummi."

Salt Spring's large Roland family, a talented and fun-loving clan, are hosting the event. Cathy Roland is a firebrand who can usually be found belting out blues at Vancouver Island pubs and clubs. Today, however, with her three sisters, she croons soft South Seas ballads and love songs in Hawaiian and English. Backing her on bass is brother Dave, also a popular local musician. Down on the beach another brother, Herk Roland, who has continued a family tradition of logging and commercial fishing, tends the roasting pig.

Later, following the gala feast, three generations of British Columbia's Messer and Johnston families take over the entertainment. The part-Hawaiian, part-Tahitian descendants of Fraser steamboat Captain Owen Browne treat the crowd to a colourful and rousing display of hula dancing. Tito and Shannon Messer, in bright red and blue muumuus and garlanded hair, weave provocative images with their hands. They even lure a gaggle of men to get up and join them in a schmaltzy fishing dance. And then, the show-stopper. Gorgeous young Natasha Johnston, in a low-slung wrap and a halter of coconut shells, pops eyeballs with a fiery and seductive Tahitian drum dance.

❊　❊　❊

The descendants of Maria Mahoy slip away from the luau to dedicate a family commemorative stone. Fully assimilated into the Canadian mainstream, they are civil servants and university students, health care workers and pensioners. The most prominent is B.C.'s former finance minister, Mel Couvelier, one of Maria Mahoy's many great-grandchildren. After five generations, some of them still look distinctly Polynesian, others hardly at all. "There's a lot of cream in the coffee," quips Karey Litton.

They gather at nearby St. Paul's Church, where Maria and her daughter Mary Jane Fisher are buried—somewhere—but the old grave markers have been moved and lost over the years. Stan Bell tells how his grandmother, Mary Jane Fisher, used to row in from Russell Island to take them

Larry Bell unveils plaque commemorating the Kanakas of the Gulf Islands. At right, Don Watt and Tony Farr of the Salt Spring Island Historical Society.
(Tom Koppel)

to church, bringing flowers for the altar and always towing a fishing line. "She never missed a chance to fish."

The stone is dedicated to Violet Bell, Maria Mahoy's granddaughter, who was born on Russell Island in 1908 and died in Victoria in 1993. Larry Bell tells a favourite family story, about how when Violet, his mother, was born the air on Russell Island was thick with hummingbirds. Maria Mahoy told everyone this meant that hummingbirds were Violet's *tamanos* or guardian spirits, and so they remained during all of her long life.

The little group sings "Amazing Grace," poses for a few pictures, and drifts back to the luau. But they leave behind one more legacy of the Kanaka presence on the Northwest Coast. There, engraved on a corner of the stone, is a tiny hummingbird.

Notes

Introduction

1. The word *kanaka* was widely used in the nineteenth century in the Pacific to refer to Pacific Islanders in general, not just Hawaiians. At least in its early use, it was not a derogatory term, and never had pejorative connotations in Canada, where it was routinely appended to names on census forms and voters' lists. In present-day Melanesian Pidgin, however, it has a somewhat pejorative sense, especially in the phrase "bush kanaka," meaning a backward, uncivilized person. Large numbers of Melanesians worked on sugar plantations in Queensland, Australia, in the nineteenth century. Some of their descendants there today are known as Kanakas. The French form, *canaque*, was used to refer to the indigenous Melanesians of New Caledonia. This may have had a somewhat derogatory sense at one time, but it has now been taken over by Melanesian nationalists, who refer to themselves as Kanaks and to the country as Kanaky.

   I am indebted to Professor Ross Clark, Department of Anthropology, University of Auckland, New Zealand, for the information on Polynesian and Melanesian languages and Pidgin English in the Pacific. Letter from Clark, 29 December 1990.

2. Although Kanakas constituted between thirty and sixty percent of the work force at most west coast Hudson's Bay Company posts, they are not mentioned by Peter C. Newman in his voluminous history of the HBC, *Company of Adventurers* (Markham, Ont.: Penguin, 1987). George Woodcock gives them some attention in his *British Columbia, A History of the Province* (Vancouver: Douglas & McIntyre, 1990). Jean Barman, in *The West Beyond the West, A History of British Columbia* (Toronto: University of Toronto Press, 1991) gives concise but accurate glimpses of the Kanakas in early B.C. society, especially their interrelationship with native Indians.

Chapter 1

1. Beth Hill, *The Remarkable World of Frances Barkley: 1769–1845* (Sidney, B.C.: Gray's, 1978), 22.
2. John Meares, *Voyages Made in the Years 1788 and 1789 . . .* (London: 1790), 9–10, cited in Janice K. Duncan, *Minority Without a Champion, Kanakas on the Pacific Coast, 1788–1850* (Portland: Oregon Historical Society, 1972), 3.
3. Ibid., journal entry for 5 February 1788.
4. Hill, *Frances Barkley*, 22.
5. Janice K. Duncan, "Kanaka World Travelers and Fur Company Employees, 1785–1860," *Hawaiian Journal of History*, vol. 7 (1973), 94.
6. Meares, *Voyages*, 27, cited in Hill, *Frances Barkley*, 54–55.
7. Francine du Plessix Gray, *Hawaii: The Sugar-Coated Fortress* (New York: Random House, 1972), 41.

Chapter 2

1. Gabriel Franchere, *The Journal of Gabriel Franchere*, ed. W. Kaye Lamb (Toronto: Champlain Society, 1969), 70.
2. Ed Towse, "Some Hawaiians Abroad," Papers of the Hawaiian Historical Society, no. 11 (1904), 11.
3. Beth Hill, *The Remarkable World of Frances Barkley: 1769–1845* (Sidney, B.C.: Gray's, 1978), 133.
4. Franchere, *Journal*, 59–60.
5. Richard Henry Dana Jr., *Two Years Before the Mast and Twenty-Four Years After* (New York: P. F. Collier, 1909), 62.
6. Alexander Ross, *Adventures of the First Settlers On the Oregon and Columbia River* (London: Smith, Elder & Co., 1849), 69–70.
7. Franchere, *Journal*, 75.
8. Ross, *Adventures of First Settlers*, 80–81.
9. Franchere, *Journal*, 90.
10. Ross, *Adventures of First Settlers*, 123–24.

11. Alexander Ross, *The Fur Hunters of the Far West* (London: 1855), 193, cited in David Kittleson, "Hawaiians and Fur Traders," *Hawaii Historical Review*, vol. 1, no. 2 (January 1963), 18.
12. Ross Cox, *Adventures on the Columbia River*, 2 vols. (London: H. Colburn, 1831), 11.
13. Ibid., 262–63.
14. Janice K. Duncan, "Kanaka World Travelers and Fur Company Employees, 1785–1860," *Hawaiian Journal of History*, vol. 7 (1973), 98.

Chapter 3

1. George Simpson, *Fur Trade and Empire* (Cambridge: 1931), 91, cited in David Kittleson, "Hawaiians and Fur Traders," *Hawaii Historical Review*, vol. 1, no. 2 (January 1963), 18.
2. Agreement of 11 February 1840, cited in Thomas G. Thrum, "History of the Hudson's Bay Company's Agency in Honolulu," Hawaiian Hist. Soc. Annual Report (18th), 1910, 39–40.
3. Tally of Kanaka servants based on HBC employment records. Years surveyed are from Outfit 1842 through 1870 for the Columbia (and later Western) Department. HBCA files surveyed are B.223/g/7-17; B.226/g/1-18; B.223/d/152, 156, 157, 159, 161, 162, 169, 173, 176, 184, 187, 195; B/15/a.
4. HBCA B.223/d/162. According to another researcher's statistical breakdown of HBC employees, in January to June 1846 the total number of Hawaiians serving south of the forty-ninth parallel (the eventual Canada-U.S. border) was 152. This number included one teacher, one cooper, one woodcutter (among ship's crew), one sawyer, two shepherds, one middleman, and 145 labourers (four of whom were among ship crews). The rest of the employees consisted of 40 Englishmen, 74 Scots (largely from the Orkney, Shetland, and Hebrides Islands), one Frenchman, 10 Canadians of British origin, 70 Canadians of French origin, 11 Iroquois Indians, and 42 "natives" of Rupert's Land (the HBC's chartered territory), most of them "half-breeds." The figures are based on HBCA B.239/l/16 and B.239/g/85. O. O. Winther, "The British in Oregon Country," *Pacific Northwest Quarterly* (October 1967), 186–87.
5. Teacher/minister William Kaulehelehe, later called an "assistant" in Victoria, was an exception, but he was taken on in a special capacity from the start.
6. Jean M. Cole, *Exile in the Wilderness* (Don Mills, Ont.: Burns & MacEachern, 1979), 160.
7. James R. Gibson, *Farming the Frontier: The Agricultural Opening of the Oregon Country, 1786–1846* (Vancouver: UBC Press, 1985), 37.
8. Yvonne Mearns Klan, "Kanaka William," *The Beaver* (Spring 1979), 40.
9. Ibid., 39.
10. Herbert Beaver, *Reports and Letters of Herbert Beaver 1836–1838*, ed. Thomas E. Jessett (Portland: Champoeg Press, 1959), 86.
11. Klan, "Kanaka William," 39.
12. Beaver, *Reports and Letters*, 131.
13. *The Friend* (Honolulu), 2 February 1863, 10.
14. Klan, "Kanaka William," 40.
15. Ibid., 41.
16. Ibid.
17. Ibid.
18. David Kittleson, "John Coxe: Hawaii's First Soldier of Fortune," *Hawaii Historical Review*, vol. 1 (January 1965), 196.
19. *Times* (London), 15 July 1824.
20. Rev. George Henry Atkinson, "Diary of Rev. George Henry Atkinson, D.D., 1847–1858," ed. Ruth E. Rockwood, *Oregon Historical Quarterly*, vol. 40, 185, cited in Janice K. Duncan, "Minority Without a Champion: The Kanaka Contribution to the Western United States, 1750–1900" (master's thesis, Portland State University, 1972), 64.
21. James R. Anderson, "Notes and Comments on Early Days and Events in British Columbia, Washington and Oregon," Mss. in PABC, 1925, 209–10, cited in Derek Pethick, *Victoria: The Fort* (Vancouver: Mitchell, 1968), 138, n. 12.
22. Beatrice Hamilton, *Salt Spring Island*, (Vancouver: Mitchell, 1969), 82.

Chapter 4

1. F. G. Young, ed., *The Correspondence and Journals of Captain Nathaniel J. Wyeth 1831–6* (Sources of Oregon History, pts. 3–6, Eugene, 1899), journal entry 15 September 1834, cited in Janice K. Duncan, *Minority Without a Champion: Kanakas on the Pacific Coast* (Portland: Oregon Historical Society, 1972), 8.
2. Young, ed., *Captain Wyeth,* journal entry 6 February 1835, cited in Duncan, *Minority*, 8.
3. *Oregon Spectator* 5 February 1846, cited in Janice K. Duncan, "Minority Without A Champion: The Kanaka Contribution to the Western United States, 1750–1900" (master's thesis, Portland State University, 1972), 78.
4. *The Friend* (Honolulu), 4 September 1844, 79.
5. Cited in Derek Pethick, *Victoria: The Fort* (Vancouver: Mitchell, 1968), 80.
6. Robert Lloyd Webb, *On the Northwest: Commercial Whaling in the Pacific Northwest, 1790–1967* (Vancouver: UBC Press, 1988), 30–31.
7. Sir George Simpson, *Narrative of a Journey Around the World, During the Years 1841 and 1842* (London: H. Colburn, 1847) vol. 2, 15, cited in Susan Kardas, "The People Bought This and the Clatsop Became Rich" (A View of Nineteenth Century Fur Trade Relationships on the Lower Columbia Between Chinookan Speakers, Whites and Kanakas) (Ph.D. diss., Bryn Mawr College, Pennsylvania, April 1971), 107.
8. Greer, Richard A. "Wandering Kamaainas: Notes on Hawaiian Emigration Before 1848," *Journal of the West,* vol. 6, no. 2 (April 1967), 224.
9. Duncan, "Minority" (thesis), 91.
10. *The Friend* (Honolulu), 1 September 1865, cited in Duncan, "Minority" (thesis), 92.
11. Ibid., 15 November 1849, cited in Duncan, "Minority" (thesis), 82.
12. Richard Henry Dana Jr., *Two Years Before the Mast and Twenty-Four Years After* (New York: P. F. Collier, 1909), 146.
13. Ibid., 146–47.
14. Ibid., 150.
15. Ibid., 151.
16. Ibid.
17. Ibid., 152.
18. Ibid., 154.
19. Ibid., 172.
20. Ibid., 179.
21. Ibid., 407.

Chapter 5

1. Donald E. Waite, *The Langley Story* (Maple Ridge, B.C.: Don Waite Publishing, 1977), 2.
2. Gilbert Malcolm Sproat, "Career of a Scotch Boy Who Became Hon. John Tod," chap. 23, excerpted in Victoria *Daily Times,* 23 December 1905.
3. *Fort Langley Journal,* typescript copy on display at Fort, 10–21.
4. Ibid., 22.
5. Cited in James R. Gibson, *Farming the Frontier: The Agricultural Opening of the Oregon Country, 1786–1846* (Vancouver: UBC Press, 1985), 48.
6. Cited in Wellwood R. Johnson, *Legend of Langley* (Langley: Langley Centennial Committee, 1958), 10.
7. Waite, *Langley,* 9.
8. Allard reminiscences, quoted in Jamie Morton, "Fort Langley: An Overview of the Operations of a Diversified Fur Trade Post 1848 to 1858 and the Physical Context in 1858," Canadian Parks Service, microfiche report series no. 340, 274.
9. CVA, Add. Mss. 205.
10. Allard reminiscences, in Mary K. Cullen, "The History of Fort Langley," Canadian Historical Sites, Occasional Papers in Archaeology and History, no. 20 (Ottawa: National Historic Parks and Sites Branch 1979), appendix C, 90.
11. Ibid.
12. Ibid.
13. Janice K. Duncan, "Kanaka World Travelers and Fur Company Employees, 1785–1860," *Hawaiian Journal of History,* vol. 7 (1973), 106.
14. E. Momilani Naughton, "Hawaiians in the Fur Trade: Cultural Influences on the Northwest Coast, 1811–1875" (master's thesis, Western Washington University, Bellingham, August 1983), 55.

Chapter 6

1. William Fraser Tolmie, *The Journals of William Fraser Tolmie, Physician and Fur Trader* (Vancouver: Mitchell Press, 1963), 300, 311.
2. James R. Gibson, *Farming the Frontier: The Agricultural Opening of the Oregon Country, 1786–1846* (Vancouver: UBC Press, 1985), 60.
3. Roderick Finlayson, *Biography of Roderick Finlayson* (Victoria: 1891), 8.
4. Dr. J. S. Helmcken, quoted in Jamie Morton, "Fort Langley: An Overview of the Operations of A Diversified Fur Trade Post 1848 to 1858 and The Physical Context in 1858," Canadian Parks Service, microfiche report series no. 340, 284; and Fort Rupert Journal, 4 September 1849, HBCA B.185/a/1, quoted in Barry M. Gough, *Gunboat Frontier: British Maritime Authority and Northwest Coast Indians 1846–1890* (Vancouver: UBC Press, 1984), 38.
5. Lynne Bowen, *Three Dollar Dreams* (Lantzville, B.C.: Oolichan, 1987), 32.
6. Frieda Klippenstein, "The Role of the Carrier in the Fur Trade," Parks Canada, n.d., 35.
7. HBCA, B.188/e/1 fo. 3, cited in Klippenstein, "The Role of the Carrier," 36.
8. Quoted in Klippenstein, "The Role of the Carrier," 81.

Chapter 7

1. Yvonne Mearns Klan, "Kanaka William," *The Beaver* (Spring 1979), 42.
2. Janice K. Duncan, *Minority Without a Champion: Kanakas on the Pacific Coast* (Portland: Oregon Historical Society, 1972), 14.
3. Richard H. Dillon, "Kanaka Colonies in California," *Pacific Historical Review,* vol. 24 (1955), 18.
4. Duncan, *Minority,* 15. The California legislature also prohibited the state's small population of free blacks from giving evidence in court against whites and permitted the arrest of fugitive slaves by their Southern white owners. In 1858 a bill was introduced to prohibit the immigration to California of "free negroes and other obnoxious persons."

This led to the exodus of some four hundred American blacks to British Columbia. See Crawford Killian, *Go Do Some Great Thing* (Vancouver: Douglas & McIntyre, 1978), 15.
5. Duncan, *Minority,* 16.
6. Ibid., 18.
7. Dillon, "Kanaka Colonies," 19–20.
8. Ibid., 25.

Chapter 8

1. W. H. Hills, Journal, Mss. 1436/1 (Mitchell Library, Sydney, Australia), 138, cited in Barry M. Gough, *Gunboat Frontier, British Maritime Authority and Northwest Coast Indians, 1846–1890* (Vancouver: UBC Press, 1984), 25.
2. Charles Lillard, *Seven Shillings a Year* (Ganges, B.C.: Horsdal & Schubart, 1986), 142.
3. Derek Pethick, *Victoria: The Fort* (Vancouver: Mitchell, 1968), 35.
4. David Richardson, *Pig War Islands* (Eastsound, Wash.: Orcas Publishing, 1971), 40.
5. B. A. McKelvie and Willard E. Ireland, "The Victoria Voltigeurs," *British Columbia Historical Quarterly,* vol. 20 (1956), nos. 3 and 4, 221.
6. Ibid., 227.
7. Douglas to William G. Smith, 1 April 1855, Fort Victoria, Correspondence Outward to HBC on affairs of Vancouver Island Colony, 11 December 1855 to 8 July 1859, quoted in McKelvie and Ireland, "Victoria Voltigeurs," 237.
8. Harry Gregson, *A History of Victoria, 1842–1970* (Vancouver: J. J. Douglas, 1970), 13.
9. Ibid., 6.
10. Ibid., 21.
11. *British Colonist* (Victoria), 12 May 1860, 3.
12. *Daily British Colonist* and *Victoria Chronicle* (Victoria), 18 June 1873, 3.
13. *Daily British Colonist* (Victoria), January 1864, quoted in *The B.C. Genealogist,* vol. 2, no. 3 (Autumn 1982), 68.

Chapter 9

1. E. Momilani Naughton, "Hawaiians in the Fur Trade: Cultural Influences on the Northwest Coast, 1811–1875" (master's thesis, Western Washington University,

Bellingham, August 1983), 49–50, letter translated by Paulani Case. The letter was probably written for Naukana, who was said to be illiterate.

2. *British Columbia & Victoria Directory,* 1863, 50.

3. Rithet to Foreign Office, 5 September 1879, Hawaiian State Archives.

4. James G. Swan (consul Port Townsend) to Foreign Office, 13 May, 13 August, and 27 September 1886 and attachments from Jefferson County Auditor, Hawaiian State Archives.

5. *Daily British Colonist* (Victoria), 19 September 1860; 2, 21 September 1860, 2; 25 September 1860, 3; and 20 October 1860, 3; and J. K. Nesbitt, "Victorians Agog for Royal Visit," *Colonist* (Victoria), 21 August 1960, Magazine, 16.

6. Gabriel Franchere, *Adventures at Astoria, 1810–1814* (Norman: University of Oklahoma Press, 1967), 34, quoted in Susan Kardas, "The People Bought This And The Clatsop Became Rich" (A View of Nineteenth Century Fur Trade Relationships on the Lower Columbia between Chinookan Speakers, Whites, and Kanakas) (Ph.D. diss. Bryn Mawr College, Pennsylvania, April 1971), 106.

7. Kardas, "The People Bought This," 108.

8. Ibid., 109.

9. Francine du Plessix Gray, *Hawaii: The Sugar-Coated Fortress* (New York: Random House, 1972), 35.

10. Robert C. Schmitt, "Population Characteristcs of Hawaii, 1778–1850," *Hawaii Historical Review,* vol. 1, no. 2 (April 1965), 199.

11. Gray, *Hawaii,* 63.

Chapter 10

1. W. J. Illerbrun, "Kanaka Pete," *Hawaiian Journal of History,* vol. 6 (1972), 156.

2. Ibid., 159.

3. Ibid., 162–63.

4. *Daily British Colonist* and *Victoria Chronicle* (Victoria), 11 March 1969, cited in Illerbrun, "Kanaka Pete," 164.

5. David Richardson, *Pig War Islands* (Eastsound, Wash.: Orcas Publishing, 1971), 174.

Chapter 11

1. Dorothy Blakey Smith, ed., "The Journal of Arthur Thomas Bushby 1858–1859," *British Columbia Historical Quarterly* (January–October, 1957–58), 127, quoted in Jamie Morton, "Fort Langley: An Overview of the Operations of A Diversified Fur Trade Post 1848 to 1858 and The Physical Context in 1858," Canadian Parks Service, microfiche report series no. 340, 288.

2. Douglas to Yale, 1 July 1857, quoted in Morton, "Fort Langley," 288.

3. R. Bouchard and D. Kennedy, "Tsawwassen Ethnography and Ethnohistory," report for B.C. Ministry of Highways (February 1991 in typescript), 38.

4. *Daily World* (Vancouver), 10 August 1915, clipping in CVA file on Kanaka Creek.

5. Charles A. Miller, *Valley of the Stave* (Surrey, B.C.: Hancock House, 1981), 21–22.

6. Ibid., 32.

Chapter 12

1. CVA, Add. Mss. 54 (CVA 54), conversation with William Nahanee, 12 September 1941.

2. M. Bate, "A Story of Olden Days Graphically Told By One Who Knows," *Daily Herald* (Nanaimo) [n.d., circa 1900–1910].

3. Alan Morley, *Vancouver: From Milltown to Metropolis* (Vancouver: Mitchell Press, 1961), 67.

4. CVA 54, letter of Mary Eihu to Vancouver mayor and city council, 1 October 1899.

5. CVA 54, Mrs. R. D. Smith, 2 April 1937.

6. Hilda Mortimer, *You Call Me Chief: Impressions of the Life of Chief Dan George* (Toronto: Doubleday, 1981), 115.

7. Ibid., 115–16.

8. *Vancouver Sun,* Cards of Thanks, 26 April 1989.

9. Terry Glavin, "Legacy of Forgotten Hawaiians Seen Throughout BC Coast," *Vancouver Sun,* 25 May 1991, A5.

10. CVA 54, Alice Crakanthorp, 22 May 1940.

11. Ibid.

12. *Vancouver Sun,* 3 January 1957.

Chapter 13

1. *Daily British Colonist* and *Victoria Chronicle* (Victoria), 28 April 1870.
2. Dorothea M. Scarfe Croquet, "Father Leon Fouquet," 1958, Handwritten ms. in PABC.
3. Obituary, *Pioneer Journal* (Alert Bay), 9 May 1956.
4. *Daily British Colonist* (Victoria), 17 March 1880, 2.
5. Art Downs, *Paddlewheels on the Frontier*, vol. 1 (Surrey, B.C.: Foremost Publishing, 1971), 1.
6. Ibid., 53.
7. Ibid., 58.

Chapter 14

1. Reverend Ebenezer Robson, Diaries, 1 February 1861, ms. in PABC, quoted in A. F. Flucke, "Early Days on Saltspring Island," *British Columbia Historical Quarterly*, vol. 15, nos. 3 and 4, 1951, 190.
2. John A. Caldwell, letter to Jane Emily Wood, 6 March 1947, based on information provided by Ernest Harrison, "born here in 1867, and now the oldest living man born on Salt Spring Island." Copy in author's possession.
3. Application for government survey accompanying pre-emption document, M. Melia Lane, "Migration of Hawaiians to Coastal BC, 1810–1869" (master's thesis, University of Hawaii, Honolulu, 1985), 80.
4. Letter of 8 June 1885 from W. F. Tolmie to Henry Fry, J.P., PABC, copy in Salt Spring Island Archives.
5. Mabel Davis interview transcript, PABC tape 800, tape 2, track 1, 9.
6. Beatrice Hamilton, *Salt Spring Island* (Vancouver: Mitchell Press, 1969), 83–84.

Chapter 15

1. Mary Cooke, "Hawaiian Colony Found in Canada," *Honolulu Advertiser*, 29 June 1971.
2. Sally Jo Moon, "Aloha Alive and Well in British Columbia," *Honolulu Star-Bulletin*, 14 August 1971, B1.
3. Paul Roland, PABC tape 3807-1.
4. Beatrice Hamilton, *Salt Spring Island* (Vancouver: Mitchell Press, 1969), 83.
5. Mabel Davis, PABC tape 800, transcript, 10.
6. Jack Roland, PABC tape 3807-1.
7. "Pioneer Kanaka Dies at Age of 96," *Daily Colonist* (Victoria), 23 December 1909.
8. Interview with Laura Roland, 9 October 1987.
9. Jack Roland, PABC tape 3807-1.
10. Laura Roland interview.
11. Moon, "Aloha Alive."

Chapter 16

1. Elma Rowbotham, "Schoolhouse Memories," *Daily Colonist* (Victoria), 11 June 1973, Magazine, 13.
2. Interview with Violet Bell, 16 November 1990.
3. Interview with Harry Roberts, 29 October 1987.
4. Ibid.

Bibliography

Fully annotated manuscripts have been deposited with the Salt Spring Island Archives, the Hudson's Bay Company Archives, and Special Collections, McPherson Library, University of Victoria.

Publications

Barman, Jean. *The West Beyond the West, A History of British Columbia.* Toronto: University of Toronto Press, 1991.

Bate, M. "A Story of Olden Days Graphically Told by One Who Knows." *Daily Herald* (Nanaimo) [n.d., circa 1900–1910].

Beaver, Herbert. *Reports and Letters of Herbert Beaver 1836–1838.* (Thomas E. Jessett, ed.) Portland: Champoeg Press, 1959.

Bouchard, R. and D. Kennedy. "Tsawwassen Ethnography and Ethnohistory." Report for B.C. Ministry of Highways, typescript, February 1991.

Bowen, Lynne. *Three Dollar Dreams.* Lantzville, B.C.: Oolichan, 1987.

British Columbia and Victoria Directory, 1863.

Cole, Jean M. *Exile in the Wilderness (The Life of Chief Factor Archibald McDonald, 1790–1853).* Don Mills, Ont.: Burns & MacEachern, 1979.

Cooke, Mary. "Hawaiian Colony Found in Canada." *Honolulu Advertiser,* 29 June 1971.

Cox, Ross. *Adventures on the Columbia River.* 2 vols. London: H. Colburn & R. Bentley, 1831.

Croquet, Dorothea M. Scarfe. "Father Leon Fouquet." Handwritten ms. in PABC, 1958.

Cullen, Mary K. "The History of Fort Langley." Canadian Historic Sites, Occasional Papers in Archaeology and History, no. 20. Ottawa: National Historic Parks and Sites Branch, 1979.

Dana, Richard Henry Jr. *Two Years Before the Mast and Twenty-Four Years After.* New York: P. F. Collier, 1909.

Dillon, Richard H. "Kanaka Colonies in California." *Pacific Historical Review,* vol. 24 (1955), 17–23.

Downs, Art. *Paddlewheels on the Frontier.* vol. 1. Surrey, B.C.: Foremost, 1971.

Duncan, Janice K. "Kanaka World Travelers and Fur Company Employees, 1785–1860," *Hawaiian Journal of History,* vol. 7 (1973), 93–111.

———. *Minority Without a Champion, Kanakas on the Pacific Coast, 1788–1850.* Portland: Oregon Historical Society, 1972.

———. "Minority Without a Champion: The Kanaka Contribution to the Western United States, 1750–1900." Master's thesis, Portland State University, 1972.

Finlayson, Roderick. *Biography of Roderick Finlayson* (Victoria: 1891).

Flucke, A. F. "Early Days on Saltspring Island," *British Columbia Historical Quarterly,* vol. 15, nos. 3 and 4, 1951.

Franchere, Gabriel. *The Journal of Gabriel Franchere.* Ed. W. Kaye Lamb. Toronto: Champlain Society, 1969.

Gibson, James R. *Farming the Frontier: The Agricultural Opening of the Oregon Country, 1786–1846.* Vancouver: UBC Press, 1985.

Glavin, Terry. "Legacy of Forgotten Hawaiians Seen Throughout BC Coast." *Vancouver Sun,* 25 May 1991, A5.

Gough, Barry M. *Gunboat Frontier: British Maritime Authority and Northwest Coast Indians 1846–1890.* Vancouver: UBC Press, 1984.

Gray, Francine du Plessix. *Hawaii: The Sugar-Coated Fortress.* New York: Random House, 1972.

Greer, Richard A. "Wandering Kamaainas: Notes on Hawaiian Emigration Before 1848." *Journal of the West,* vol. 6, no. 2 (April 1967).

Gregson, Harry. *A History of Victoria, 1842–1970.* Vancouver: J. J. Douglas, 1970.

Hamilton, Bea. "Dream That Came True." *Daily Colonist* (Victoria) 31 October 1971.

Hamilton, Beatrice. *Salt Spring Island*. Vancouver: Mitchell, 1969.

Hill, Beth. *The Remarkable World of Frances Barkley: 1769–1845*. Sidney, B.C.: Gray's, 1978.

Illerbrun, W. J. "Kanaka Pete." *Hawaii Journal of History*, vol. 6 (1972), 156–66.

Johnson, Wellwood R. *Legend of Langley*. Langley: Langley Centennial Committee, 1958.

Kardas, Susan. "The People Bought This and the Clatsop Became Rich" (A View of Nineteenth Century Fur Trade Relationships on the Lower Columbia Between Chinookan Speakers, Whites and Kanakas.) Ph.D. diss., Bryn Mawr College, Pennsylvania, April 1971.

Kittleson, David. "John Coxe: Hawaii's First Soldier of Fortune." *Hawaii Historical Review*, vol. 1 (January 1965).

————. "Hawaiians and Fur Traders." *Hawaii Historical Review*, vol. 1, no. 2 (January 1963).

Klan, Yvonne Mearns. "Kanaka William." *The Beaver*. Outfit 309: 4 (Spring 1979), 38–43.

Klippenstein, Frieda. "The Role of the Carrier in the Fur Trade." Parks Canada, n.d.

Lane, M. Melia. "Migration of Hawaiians to Coastal B.C., 1810–1869." Master's thesis, University of Hawaii, Honolulu, 1985.

Lillard, Charles. *Seven Shillings a Year*. Ganges, B.C.: Horsdal & Schubart, 1986.

Maclachlan, Morag. "The Founding of Fort Langley." in E. Blanche Norcross, ed., *The Company on the Coast*. Nanaimo: Nanaimo Hist. Soc., 1983.

McKelvie, B. A. and Willard E. Ireland. "The Victoria Voltigeurs." *British Columbia Historical Quarterly*, vol. 20 (1956), nos. 3 and 4.

Miller, Charles A. *Valley of the Stave*. Surrey, B.C.: Hancock House, 1981.

Moon, Sally Jo. "Aloha Alive and Well in British Columbia." *Honolulu Star-Bulletin*, 14 August 1971, B1.

Morley, Alan. *Vancouver: From Milltown to Metropolis*. Vancouver: Mitchell, 1961.

Mortimer, Hilda. *You Call Me Chief: Impressions of the Life of Chief Dan George*. Toronto: Doubleday, 1981.

Morton, Jamie. "Fort Langley: An Overview of the Operations of a Diversified Fur Trade Post 1848 to 1858 and the Physical Context in 1858." Canadian Parks Service, microfiche report series no. 340.

Naughton, E. Momilani. "Hawaiians in the Fur Trade: Cultural Influence on the Northwest Coast, 1811–1875." Master's thesis, Western Washington University, Bellingham, August 1983.

Nesbitt, J. K. "Victorians Agog for Royal Visit." *Daily Colonist* (Victoria), 21 August 1960, Magazine, 16.

Newman, Peter C. *Company of Adventurers*. Markham, Ont.: Penguin, 1987.

Pethick, Derek. *Victoria: The Fort*. Vancouver: Mitchell, 1968.

"Public Meeting at Cassiar," *Daily British Colonist* (Victoria), 17 March 1880, 2.

Richardson, David. *Pig War Islands*. Eastsound, Wash.: Orcas Publishing, 1971.

Ross, Alexander. *Adventures of the First Settlers on the Oregon and Columbia River*. London: Smith, Elder & Co., 1849.

Rowbotham, Elma. "Schoolhouse Memories," *Daily Colonist* (Victoria), 11 June 1973, Magazine, 13.

Schmitt, Robert C. "Population Characteristics of Hawaii, 1778–1850." *Hawaii Historical Review*, vol. 1, no. 2 (April 1965).

Sproat, Gilbert Malcolm. "Career of a Scotch Boy Who Became Hon. John Tod." Chap. 23, excerpted in Victoria *Daily Times*, 23 December 1905.

Thrum, Thomas G. "History of the Hudson's Bay Company's Agency in Honolulu." Hawaiian Hist. Soc. Annual Report (18th), 1910.

Tolmie, William Fraser. *The Journals of William Fraser Tolmie, Physician and Fur Trader*. Vancouver: Mitchell, 1963.

Towse, Ed. "Some Hawaiians Abroad." Papers of the Hawaiian Historical Society, no. 11, 1904.

Waite, Donald E. *The Langley Story, Illustrated*. Maple Ridge, B.C.: Don Waite Publishing, 1977.

Webb, Robert Lloyd. *On the Northwest: Commercial Whaling in the Pacific Northwest, 1790–1967.* Vancouver: UBC Press, 1988.

Winther, O. O. "The British in the Oregon Country." *Pacific Northwest Quarterly,* vol. 58, no. 4, October 1967, 179–87.

Woodcock, George. *British Columbia, A History of the Province.* Vancouver: Douglas & McIntyre, 1990.

Newspapers

Daily Colonist (Victoria)—also *British Colonist, Daily British Colonist,* and *Daily British Colonist and Victoria Chronicle.* 12 May 1860; 19 September 1860; 21 September 1860; 20 October 1860; 28 April 1870; 23 December 1909.

Daily World (Vancouver), 10 August 1915.

The Friend (Honolulu), 4 September 1844; 1 October 1849; 2 February 1863.

Pioneer Journal (Alert Bay), 9 May 1956.

Times (London), 15 July 1824.

Vancouver Sun, 3 January 1957; 26 April 1989.

Other Sources

B.C. Genealogist, vol. 2, no. 3 (Autumn 1982); vol. 20, no. 1 (March 1991).

Census of Canada 1881, 1891.

Hawaiian State Archives (Honolulu). Correspondence with Hawaiian consuls in Victoria and Port Townsend, Washington.

Hudson's Bay Company Archives (HBCA). B.223/d/ 19, 28, 37, 47, 54, 61, 77, 88, 100, 121, 152, 156, 159, 161, 162, 169, 176, 184, 187, 195, District Statements and Statements of Servants, Fort Vancouver 1828–1851.

———. B.223/g/1-17, Abstracts of Servants' Accounts, Fort Vancouver (Columbia District), 1827–1862.

———. B.226/g/1-18, Abstracts of Servants' Accounts, Fort Victoria, (Western Department) 1853–1871.

———. B. 15/a/1-2 Post Journals, Bellevue Sheep Farm, 1854–1862.

Provincial Archives of British Columbia (PABC). Add Mss 520, Box 3, File 1 Baptismal register of Fort Vancouver and Fort Victoria, 1836–1859; File 6 Parish Register, Burials Fort Victoria 1855–1858; File 7 Christ Church Cathedral, Victoria, Parish Register, Burials 1859–1872.

———. GR 766, Pre-emptions 1861–1885.

———. Aural history tapes 800, 801, 802, 3807.

Vancouver City Archives, Add. Mss 54, Add. Mss 205.

Interviews with (or personal communications from) Violet Bell, Jackie Hembruff, Tom Johnston, Margaret Lee, Karey Litton, Wendy Maurer, Donna Miranda, Carey Myers, James Nahanee, Harry Roberts, Sherry Roberts, Laura Roland.

Index

Photos are in **boldface**.

Index